Tomo Izumi

The
Crystal City Story

One Family's Experience
with the World War II
Japanese Internment Camps

Some of the material in this book first appeared in the *Crystal City Chatter* newsletter. Some of the names in this book have been changed to protect people's privacy.

The Crystal City Story:

One Family's Experience with the World War II Japanese Internment Camps.

To Rev. Kakusho and Kiyo Izumi and to Junko and Takaaki

Preface

Written by Tomoko Izumi, at age 79, this book is inspired by an article in the *Crystal City Chatter*. This newsletter, received gratefully from Sumi Shimatsu, has kept Crystal City Internment Camp friends updated with her diligent writings, news, and happenings of interest to us these many years.

In one of the newsletters, she wrote about why Crystal City Internment Camp had not been listed among the camps where the Japanese families lived during those confinement years. She found out that the camps listed were actually known as Relocation Centers, and that Crystal City was an Internment camp. Families that were confined there were going to be shipped back to Japan in exchange for Americans interned in Japan. Thus, she wrote that perhaps our Crystal City Internment Camp's existence was unknown to many Americans as well as people in other countries. Some of those who were in the Crystal City camp have visited schools to tell the story to the students that had no idea of what we went through. Tomoko decided to write about the Izumi family's experiences in the internment camp at Crystal City.

Mr. Tadashi Kanno, her good friend from Tokyo, Japan, had heard about the Japanese alien immigrants who were considered enemies of America being arrested and confined during those war years. Mr. Kanno encouraged Tomoko to write about it. He believed that many people in Japan have no idea of what those in the internment camp went through and believes that this story should be told. Thus, Tomoko's story is written in both Japanese and English.

These experiences may seem not as tragic from a child's point of view as versus whatever hardships parents, older children, adults from Mainland states, Latin American Japanese families, or German and Italian families went through. Perhaps those stories will greatly differ from those interned to be repatriated to Japan, Germany, and Italy in exchange for Americans interned in those countries.

Hopefully, her story, told from the memories and perspective of an 8-year old to the age of 12, is close to the truth of how things were. Many facts about the destinations were not told to Tomoko as a child. This is also true of information as to where people were, as well as information as to where and when families would meet, as told or untold to the wives of the internees as the families left Hawaii to join their interned husbands and fathers.

Tomoko's story is based on the recollection of her memories of "following orders" from the FBI agents. The agents accompanied her family from the time the Izumis met them at Oakland station to board the Pullman train, until the family arrived at Crystal City Internment Camp in May, 1943. The internment camp recollections are about the Izumi family and how they lived during that period of confinement.

Seventy years have elapsed. Therefore, Tomoko is unable to contact some persons named in her story. Some may have perhaps passed away, and some others now live at addresses or contact numbers unknown. She is unable to ask their permission or forgiveness to include them in her story. Instead, for some people, Tomoko has chosen to use only initials in place of first or last names. She apologizes if some of the names or events mentioned are not correct, but rather recollected as best she can from childhood memories.

Hers is a story of the family of the Rev. Kakusho Izumi, focusing mostly from Tomoko's memories and her experiences. The story spans the period from December 7, 1941, at the outbreak of World War II, up until 1951, when the Izumi family finally settled in Honolulu. Tomoko notes that, in 1957, she found some—and really only some—semblance of stability and peace of mind, from the impacts of her Father and all of the family being interned during the years of the war.

The mental anguish began the moment the FBI agents arrested her Father and continued through the family's return to Hawaii. The financial difficulties were brought on by having to repurchase household necessities and other daily livelihood needs. Income that was earned prior to the arrest was completely cut off for all those confined years, leading to the worst of hardships.

The readers will find some excerpts of events that occurred here and there, with the writings reverting back to the past, events that happened in the future and back to the present day, to continue on throughout Tomoko's story.

The readers will also find parenthetical notes referring to periods outside the time she is writing about, but relevant to the topic. Translation of Japanese words or writings of thoughts related to the subject will also be within parenthesis, and quotation marks.

Some photographs depict people whose whereabouts are unknown to Tomoko, who was unable to ask for their permission. She apologizes and asks for their forgiveness in including these photographs in her book.

This year, 2015, being the 70th anniversary of the end of World War II, Tomoko felt that the satisfaction of having to at least document what they, the Izumi family, as internees from Hawaii, went through during those 4 years was worthwhile.

Nancy Rathbun Scott

Dedication

I would like to dedicate my book to my parents, Rev. Kakusho and Kiyo Izumi, to my sister, Junko and brother, Takaaki. They played very important and unending roles in my life as a child and as I grew up to adulthood, loving and protecting me and always being there to support me whenever I needed them.

I would also like to dedicate this book to the rest of my siblings, Megumi, who had to live in Japan since she was six years old and passed away there; Hiromichi, the brother just below me, talented in playing the organ and piano but died much too young; Norie, who will accept and endure with strength what comes her way; Makoto, quiet, but sang with a voice like a lark and is at rest at Punchbowl National Cemetery; Katsuyo, born in Texas when we were confined at Crystal City Internment Camp, also quiet but strong; Thomas, who suffered many ailments and incidents but survived and realized his dream of living in Las Vegas before leaving us; Duane, an educator, Athletic Director and Vice Principal of high school, loved by us all from the moment he came into our lives at birth; and our littlest, dearest and youngest, Anna, who gave and still gives us much joy, and to Nancy Scott, for all she has done to make this book possible, in my heart, she is truly also, my Li'l Sis.

This book could not be written without any one of you, it is YOUR STORY, The IZUMIS!

Acknowledgements

I would like to thank Sumi Shimatsu, whose *Crystal City Chatter* inspired me to write this book. I also thank Tadashi Kanno for encouraging and urging me to write this book in Japanese. Those in Japan may not have known what the Japanese immigrants who were considered enemies to America, went through because of World War II.

I want to thank Dr. Raymond Taniguchi, a wonderful friend, who encouraged me throughout my writings. He is very interested in history and has helped me get advice from his publisher friend in Japan regarding the Japanese version of my book.

I am very grateful to my dearest friend, Nancy Rathbun Scott, owner of Liberty Communications Group and an author of several books, for without her friendship, kind words of encouragement, advice, invaluable and tremendous help with my book after reading my preliminary writings, I would not have had the confidence to publish it. I thank her with wholehearted love and appreciation.

I am deeply grateful to Mari Ito who came, with her husband, Hidefumi, to my home many times to teach me how to insert photographs into this book. Mari's was of tremendous help in rescuing my manuscript from a computer disaster. Had she not advised me to save additional copies "just to be safe," I would have given up writing my book. To my utter dismay, the computer I had written my story on crashed and I would have lost the entire story had she not done those intermittent savings of the finished English version manuscript before editing and proofreading, as well as the yet-to-be-finished manuscript of the Japanese version of my book. Three years of my work would have been "down the drain" and I would have most likely given up writing it all over again.

I also most wholeheartedly thank Hatch and Lei Ishizu. Upon hearing that my computer was "dead" and could not even be activated to retrieve anything by the computer repair shop, the Ishizus promptly took me that very day to buy and presented me with, a new, larger-screen HP computer. From that precious gift, I could edit and proofread my English version and complete my Japanese version of the story. It was such a relief and thankfulness overflowed from my heart to both the Ishizus and Mari when she input my story into this new computer.

I would like to extend my gratitude to Rev. Satoshi Tomioka, who is serving at the Honpa Hongwanji Hawaii Betsuin, for his translations of Buddhist terminology, of the ministerial rankings, and proofreading and correcting my errors in the Japanese version of my book.

Lastly, but not the least, I want to thank Raf, my beloved husband, for his drawing of the beautiful cover, eye-catching and attention-getting, arousing the readers' interest in wanting to read my story about the wartime internment camp traumas.

I loved books and read them throughout my life and had secretly dreamt that, perhaps, someday, I, too may write a book. Thanks to all these wonderful friends, this dream has become a reality.

-- Tomo Izumi

Table of Contents

CHAPTER I

WERE AMERICAN CITIZENS ALSO CONSIDERED THEIR COUNTRY'S ENEMIES?

Air Raid! Air Raid!! Air Raid!! Thundering sounds from Japan's Zero airplanes! Bombs dropping from the skies! Fire and black smoke! Screams of excruciating pain and fear, bodies hurt and lying on the grounds, some of them are already dead! People running around as though with unseeing eyes, running helter-skelter, not knowing where or which way to run, looking for shelter! Air and submarine attacks! U.S. Navy ships sinking! Traumatic Disaster! War! War!! War!!!

On December 7, 1941, Pearl Harbor, the United States naval base in Hawaii, on the island of Oahu, was attacked by the Zero airplanes and submarines of Japan.

This was the beginning of not only our country's involvement in World War II, but, unexpectedly and unknowingly on that tragic day, the trauma that was to continue for years, also happened to many Japanese, German, and Italian families throughout America and some Latin American countries. Alien men who were ministers, teachers, and leaders with influential roles in Japanese, German, and Italian communities, or were considered to be enemies of America, without warnings or charges, were arrested by the FBI on that very night, and taken away, leaving families in a state of utter alarm, anxiety, fear, helplessness, and sadness.

Rev. Kakusho Izumi, a ("西本願寺浄土真宗) "Nishi Hongwanji Jodo Shinshu" sect of the Mahayana Buddhism, minister, and Japanese School teacher, his wife, Kiyo, and their six children, Junko (12,) Takaaki (10,) Tomoko (8,) Hiromichi (5,) Norie (3,) and Makoto (10 months,) were living at the Papaaloa Hongwanjji Mission. That Sunday, the day began with Father going to the (別院) "Betsuin", head branch temple in Hilo, for a meeting of all the ministers from the various temples of the Honpa Hongwanji Mission on the island of Hawaii. Upon hearing the shocking news of the Pearl Harbor attack by Japan, the meeting was immediately cancelled, and everyone hurried home.

Meanwhile, the Izumi children, Junko, Takaaki, Tomoko, Hiromichi, and Norie, were playing in the upstairs room. After a while, as they began going downstairs, to the surprise of the older children, Hiromichi suddenly jumped from a rather high step, and fractured his leg.

Father had not come home yet, and Mother told Takaaki to ask Mr. U, who knew medical home remedies, to come and tend to Hiromichi. Mr. U. used to come to our home several times a month, in the early evenings, to hear the teachings of The Amida Buddha while he massaged Father's shoulders and back. He pulled on Hiromichi's fractured leg, straightening the fractured bone, covered his leg with a cloth and put it in a sticky mixture of flour, vinegar, and egg white. It had a peculiar smell when wet, but as it dried, it became odorless, and hardened into a home-made cast to hold the fracture in place.

Father returned home safely, much to our relief to have him among us, as we also felt the tension in the air, be it anxiety or fear. Since Hiromichi's leg had been treated, Father felt that it could wait until tomorrow to go to the hospital, and also thought it may be better to be at home until he learned more about the situation. It was decided that he would drive Hiromichi to the plantation hospital early the next day. Little did we know or even suspect, that an unexpected heartbreaking event was to befall upon us on that fateful Sunday night.

(As things turned out, it was Takaaki who took Hiromichi to the hospital the following morning. Hiromichi was examined, and the
X-ray showed that the bone had been set correctly, and a new proper cast was put on by the plantation doctor.)

On that rather chaotic day, with all the happenings of the Japanese attack on Pearl Harbor, with Hiromichi getting hurt and treated by Mr. U., Father being at the meeting in Hilo, but returning home to us safely, we all settled down for the night. Our parents were concerned as to what might happen to the many Japanese citizens that had immigrated to America now that the two countries were at war. We were soon unknowingly, thrown into the unexpected, traumatic, happenings, which were to bring about tremendous differences to many Japanese families, putting them into sheer panic.

That very night, many Japanese leaders were arrested, and abruptly taken away from their families. The Izumis were already in bed for the night, when there was a knock on our door, and there were two FBI agents who had come to take Father away, the Captain of the Laupahoehoe Police Station, and a member of our temple, our neighbor, who spoke English and Japanese, and was the interpreter for the agents. Father was only told that he was to follow the agents, and go with them. Father asked the men to sit and wait in the parlor, changed into his suit and robe that he wears at the services held in the temple, woke Junko, Takaaki, and Tomoko, to follow him and Mother to the temple, where he performed his own funeral. We then gathered in front of the home altar, and after praying there, he told us to listen to our Mother and to help her with the care of the rest of the siblings, who were still sleeping. He was then taken into custody, carrying his briefcase with all the necessities needed to perform a home service. (He told us much later, when we were allowed a visit to see him at the Kilauea Military Army Camp in the Volcano district, that he thought he was going to be shot to death that very night, and so had performed his funeral before leaving with the FBI agents. When he reached the camp, all of the other ministers were there, but thinking they were to be questioned and sent home, they had come wearing a jacket over their pajamas. Seeing Father wearing his suit and tie, even with his home service necessities in his briefcase, they teased him, saying that it was just like Izumi to have come so well prepared. Father was 39 years old at that time).

Rev. Kakusho Izumi, 1941

Having Father, who was the main person in our lives taken away so suddenly, not knowing what happened to him, the performing of his own funeral gave us a foreboding omen, not knowing whether he was dead or alive, turned our household of six children and Mother into a sad, dark pit of anxiety, and a deep sense of loss. It must have been a horrible nightmare for our Mother, left alone with her children, without a husband and for us without a father. How were we going to survive when the breadwinner of the family was taken away, and gone from us? Who would be driving us around or looking after us? Father, whom we all relied on and who kept our family happy and secure, taking care of us so kindly and cheerfully, was taken from us that very night war was declared. Not knowing where he was or what had happened to him, added dismay to our fears and anxiety. To have him taken away from us so abruptly without any warning, or explanation, not knowing when he would return, awakened us to how much we had taken for granted the love, security, and safeness he had provided for us by just being there for us, and realized how much of a pillar he was of our home.

This was the beginning of the many more arrests that was to come, of some of the Japanese, German, and Italian aliens, who had immigrated to America and Hawaii, which was then still a territory of the United States, and to Latin America.

(Executive Order 9066 signed by President Franklin Roosevelt of the United States, on February 19, 1942, ordered the arrests, relocation, and detention, of these aliens that were thought to be enemies, and danger to our country's security. Without warning or charges, this Order allowed the FBI to abruptly take those considered Enemy Aliens in the West and East coasts from their homes, separating them from their families, and for many, losing their homes and properties they had worked so hard to earn.) (Executive Order 9066 taken from www.ourdocuments.gov)

Father was taken on December 7, 1941. Was this order already been thought of, discussed, and anticipated, as to who was to be arrested in the event America may go to war with Japan??? There must have been a list of those arrested the very night Pearl Harbor was attacked, with their whereabouts known for them to move so immediately, swiftly and quickly, to put this order into action, and even where to confine them already in preparation. (It now seemed that military camps with soldiers able to guard the internees from escaping, were the most appropriate places to put them, as Father and the rest of those that were at the Kilauea Military Army Camp, were sent to other military camps in Oklahoma and Louisiana, while Crystal City Internment Camp was being built in the desert in Texas.) Since most of the Buddhist ministers of the different Sects, and Japanese school teachers were also arrested, at my tender age, at first, I thought leaders of the Japanese communities, who had influence on the Japanese residents living in America, were arrested. (I am now wondering in our particular case, besides being influential to the members of the congregation, was it because Father had been in regular correspondence and contact by sending living expenses to Grandmother Ko from 1931, when he arrived at his new assignment at the Hongwanji temple in Maui, and even more from 1933, when our sister, Megumi, was sent to Japan to be raised by Grandmother??? The suffering and hardships we had to endure from December 7, 1941, were also endured by Grandmother and Megumi as well, whose living expenses were cut off the moment Father was arrested that night, and all contact with America's enemy, Japan, was out of the question.)

(Recently, I thought of looking for information on the internet about articles on Crystal City Internment Camp and found an article on the website, www.thc.state.tx.us about the camp, which had paragraphs relating to the arrests of Japanese, German, and Italian aliens. In those paragraphs were explanations of some of the actions that took place, when America entered into World War II. The paragraphs from the article explained what I wrote above, however, I will leave my story as is, and would like to include these paragraphs to show how the events happened on that fateful date.)

(The following paragraphs taken from the article, "Crystal City Family Internment Camp" in the Texas Historical Commission, explained how some aliens considered dangerous to the security of our country were arrested on December 7, 1941: I wrote to the Texas Historical Commission and was granted permission to include this important data in my book.)

"The government's authority over Enemy Aliens, and by circumstance, their American-born children, came from United States Code, Title 50, Section 21, Restraint, Regulation, and Removal, which allowed for the arrest and detention of Enemy Aliens during war. President Franklin D. Roosevelt's Proclamation No. 2525 on December 7, 1941 and Proclamation No. 2526 and

No. 2527 on December 8, 1941---modeled on the Enemy Alien Act of 1798---collectively stated, "All natives, citizens, denizens, or subjects of (Japan, Germany and Italy), being of the age of fourteen years and upward, who shall be in the United States and not actually naturalized, shall be liable to be apprehended, restrained, secured, and removed as alien enemies."

Prior to these presidential proclamations, the U.S. government realized the high probability that it would eventually be involved in war. In preparation, both the DOJ through the Federal Bureau of Investigation (FBI) and the State Department, utilizing the Special War Problems Program, produced Custodial Detention Lists. This system indexed thousands of people as potentially dangerous individuals in time of war and currently residing in the U.S., and Central and South America. With this questionable legal foundation in place, the FBI began arresting Enemy Aliens from Axis nations, currently residing in America, as early as the night of December 7, 1941 and placing them in detention centers. By January, 1942, all Enemy Aliens were required to register at local post offices, and they were fingerprinted, photographed, and required to carry photo-bearing Enemy Alien Registration Cards at all times.)

CHAPTER 2

HARDSHIPS LIVING WITHOUT FATHER BEGIN

Mother, who did not speak English, despaired as to how she was going to support her 6 children without Father. We, at least, had a home that belonged to the temple where we did not have to pay rent.

Our government also probably did not think that there may be children that did not know any better than to label fathers as spies, which they were not, and could not imagine what might happen to the children of the internees, whether they were American citizens or not. No amount of comfort or compensation may be given for all the unbearable hardships and sufferings to be erased or gone from those internees and relocated Japanese, Germans, Italians and Latin American aliens and their children, some of them American citizens. All of us, who had lived through those years, although in different degrees, depending on our ages, the memory of those years of confinement are never, ever to be forgotten.

(I experienced an unpleasant incident in school. The "bad boy" of the class, who seemed to enjoy making problems for the teacher, told me one day as we came back into the empty room after recess, that he had urinated on my pink sweater because my father was a Japanese spy. I had left it on the seat when I went out to play. I silently cried but was too embarrassed so I did not tell the teacher or my siblings about this. I rinsed the sweater and threw it in the laundry basket to be washed but I did not wear that sweater to school again.)

Gas masks were distributed, probably by the government, and all students carried gas masks that were kept in an olive green canvas bag with a shoulder strap. Most of us wore it slung from one shoulder with the strap diagonally across the chest to one side of the body with the gas mask hanging near the upper thigh. There were drills on putting on the gas masks at school and I can still remember the strong rubber-like odor from it.

Air raid shelters were dug underground near every home. Some of the young men of our congregation dug our air raid shelter near the laundry building and we stocked blankets and non-perishable food in it. All of the windows had to be covered at night (blackened out,) so as not to have any lights seen from the sky in case of an air raid. Even cars were not driven at night lest the headlights could be seen from the sky. I don't know if this was true elsewhere but in our little town, it was completely dark once the sun set.

I don't remember why or whether it was mandatory or not, but I do remember going to a Bible study class at the gymnasium. There was a room where the well-baby examinations were held and a kitchen next to it between the gym and the tennis court. The bible class was held in that room. Being a daughter of a Buddhist minister, I know that I would not have, on my own, opted to attend this class. The minister from the neighboring church taught the teachings to us, who else was in the class is a blank but the first verse of the song we sang each time before the lessons began remains in my memory.

"THE B-I-B-L-E"
"Oh! The B-i-b-l-e, Yes, that's the book for me
I stand alone on the word of God
The B-I-B-L-E"

(March 14, 2015. I went to the main temple to help my sister, Junko, who was in charge of the pickled vegetables sold at the annual bazaar. Although we are all Buddhists, some of the ladies there were around my age so during lunch, I mentioned the Bible class we had to attend after the attack on Pearl Harbor. A lady there said that she also went to a bible class after the war began and it was a religious class taught at the school. Because we did not have religion as a class up to that time, was this class included because of the war, bombings and casualties may perhaps happen? Or, because the Buddhist ministers were arrested, did our government feel that the Department of Education should now have some religious classes for the youngsters that used to go to Sunday school at the temples? She went to the Congregational Church for her class in Kona. We had a Christian church within walking distance from the gym in Papaaloa and the class was taught by the minister from that church. It stands to reason then, to have the class in the room at Papaaloa gym, rather than having the minister go to Kapehu School, some distance away. America, being a Christian nation, in those days, the Pledge of Allegiance to the Flag had the word, God, in it, "One nation, under God, indivisible with liberty and justice for all," but those two words were taken out years ago and religion is not presently taught in public schools. Junko, being the eldest, said that she did not attend this class because she had to do the marketing and other household chores.)

(Without the Buddhist ministers, although the parents remained staunch Buddhists, when we returned to Hawaii from the Crystal City Internment Camp, perhaps, through the influence of those bible classes, I found some of my friends, who were members of our temple had become Christians and Catholics during the war, as had some friends from the Kilauea temple. This may be true in other various Buddhist temples where the teenagers and younger children who felt the need of religious affiliation, turned to other religious sects when the Buddhist temples were no longer available because of the sudden arrests of the ministers with the outbreak of World War II. That was understandable and acceptable, as our great country of America, with our Constitution, gives its people unalienable Freedom rights, one of them being the Freedom of Religion. Thus, the arrests of the Buddhist ministers during the war had an adverse impact not only on the internees and their families, but also to some of the Japanese in different ways, like changing their religion or to suddenly be without the availabilities of going to the ministers that they used to go to for spiritual or problematic advices when needed. They, too, found themselves abruptly cut off from ministers and leaders of their Japanese community society and left alone with worries, anxieties and mental anguish. I have never thought of or asked how funerals were conducted for the Buddhist families during those war years after we left Hawaii in 1942.)

There was a veranda starting from right outside of the kitchen door that ran along the toilet, the wash basin where we washed our hands and brushed our teeth, then turned in front of the parlor, a bedroom next to it, then turned back to the other end where the stairway to the upstairs was, and ended at the door of the master bedroom. Both the heavy wood doors to the parlor and kitchen were left open because they had a lighter framed screen door inside of them. Many times, the screen doors were not tightly shut, especially when the younger siblings went in and out of them.

Makoto must have been around 11 months old since it was after Father had been arrested and taken away. Mother did not realize that he had crawled out to the veranda. Just as she discovered Makoto near the railing, before she could take a step forward, he fell through the opening between the slats that made a cross (X) and was wide enough for a baby to fall through. She saw him fall out from the veranda that was really the second floor with the temple kitchen below our house. Frantically, she ran downstairs, picked Makoto up and with her feet bare, Mother ran all the way to the plantation hospital sobbing and carrying him close to her, uncaring or unaware of the pain of running on the pebbles on the road. Fortunately, babies are soft and supple, not even knowing the danger of his fall, Makoto stayed relaxed and not stiff with fright, having fallen onto the dirt ground rather than onto the concrete walkway. Miraculously, Makoto was not hurt anywhere. Mother, who had never walked outdoors without a slipper or shoes ran to the hospital quite some distance away and walked back home barefooted. We were all in school and S.S., who had been hired since our move to Papaaloa to help with the household chores and babysitting because Mother had to teach Japanese school and had her other duties at the temple, was at home with the other younger siblings. Those of us used to going everywhere barefooted can walk on pebbles and even hot roads but it must have been painful for Mother to run barefooted on the pebbles and hot road. (There are stories how Mothers can even do miraculous things when their children are in perilous situations. I recall that Father told a story in one of his sermons about a mother who lifted the car up when her son's foot got caught under the tire while it was being raised to change the tire and had slipped off while cranking it up. Mothers become supernaturally strong without even realizing it when they see their children need rescuing from danger even if it may be life-threatening to them. Since moving to Honolulu in 1951 when we started to wear shoes whenever we went out of the house, it hurt when we tried to walk barefooted even after a short time of wearing shoes.)

One day, we were happily notified that visitations would be allowed at the Kilauea Military Army Camp on February 15, 1942, in order to say farewells to our fathers as they were going to be shipped to Oahu. The relief of knowing that Father was well and alive and still on the same island was the most wonderful, exciting news we had since he was taken away.

The night before, we all went to bed early, looking forward to meeting Father at the army camp in Volcano, a distance far away. I was too excited to sleep, closed my eyes but the thought that we could see Father kept my mind working and imagining how things would be when we finally met him again. I guess I must have dozed off for upon waking up, disappointment flooded over me at the pitch-black darkness, which told me that it was still night time. This happened several times that night when finally, the room brightened and we could get up, have breakfast, and get ready to see Father. The excitement of being able to see and talk to Father made me feel energetic even after a rather restless night which should have made me feel lethargic and tired.

Mother had asked a neighborhood young man, M.E., a member of the temple, to drive us to Volcano in our car. She ordered us children not to show any sadness or tears but to be cheerful and happy to be able to see Father and to wish him to stay healthy and well as we bid him goodbye. The cars of yore had the front seat from door to door with the gear stick with a round knob extending up from the floor. Being little, with 3 of us including M., the driver, in the front seat and Mother carrying Makoto on her lap, the rest of us sat comfortably in the back seat. (There were no seat belts in the cars in those days.) At last, we started off to drive to Volcano.

Upon arrival, we were met by soldiers, had our identifications confirmed and escorted to one of the barracks. It was a long rectangular building of one big room and the fathers had cots lined in several rows. The cots all had olive green blankets and pillows on them. The fathers were all wearing olive green-colored army fatigues. We all sat on Father's cot, sitting as close to him as possible. It was a joyful reunion and I'm sure everyone was happy to see each father looking well and now knew where they had been staying.

The other families also sat on their fathers' cots and chatted with them. Father looked well and kept on smiling as he touched our heads, carried Makoto on his lap and looked fondly at Mother. I'm sure he missed all of us but he must have felt mostly worried about what Mother was going through by herself, looking after us and feeding us. The time together seemed to just fly by and soon we were told it was time to depart. We all smiled at Father, remembering Mother's orders to not make him feel sad or worried and that we were doing fine. It was hard not to cling on to Father and to suppress the tears that hung just inside of our eyelids.

Soon after that, we were told that Father and the other internees were being transferred to Oahu.

Not knowing what to expect from one day to another, Mother decided to have a family portrait taken at the Tabata Studio. It is the only family photograph in which Father is not with us and Hiromichi leaning on one side because of his fractured leg, which was already healed. As soon as I stand in front of a camera, I pose and put on a nice smile and as usual, get teased by my siblings.

Izumi Family, 1942

CHAPTER 3

REPATRIATION: TO JAPAN, WITH FATHER

The lonely, dreary days without Father continued into August when we were notified that he and the other internees were going to be repatriated to Japan by ship, to be exchanged with Americans interned in Japan. They wanted to know if we would like to go with him. Of course, Mother's reply was yes and with only a two-day notice, she asked the help of two ladies, Mrs. I. and Mrs. J., members of the temple's Ladies Club and who always came to her aid whenever she needed them. They hurriedly packed the things we were to take with us. My older sister, Junko also helped and she and Mother stayed up all night packing. They packed the necessary things, gave away things that could not be taken, got rid of the things no one wanted. Anything that related to Japan was burned, like the beautiful Girl's Day dolls that displayed the Imperial family and the Court, Boy's Day dolls of brave warriors wearing armor, helmet and swords, portraying strength and patriotism, No one in the community wanted those Japanese-history related things also.

Mother sold our still new Plymouth car that Father had bought after coming to Papaaloa in August to Ella A., a secretary, for $250.00 which was the sum allowed per family to take regardless of the number of members any family had. This was to us, a family of seven, unfair as the wives that had no children also were allowed the same $250.00. Even I, young as I was, knew that money was necessary to buy things and so felt it was really unfair that all families, regardless of the number of people, could take the same amount of $250.00.

On August 15, 1942, we got on a bus that picked us up to take us to Hilo harbor. As we got on, there were 3 persons already in the bus. As we proceeded on to Hilo, the bus stopped to pick up Mrs. O. and her baby son from Honohina Hongwanji Mission, at the next stop, Mrs. M. and her two sons from the Hakalau Jodo Mission, the O. family, Mrs. O., her two daughters, and her two sons, also from Hakalau. Other family members of the internees from the Big Island and our busload got onto an Inter-Island ship in Hilo and sailed to Honolulu. We were taken by an army bus to Fort Armstrong on Ala Moana Boulevard where we spent a few nights while every families' luggage was inspected and some of the things were confiscated.

Several days later, all of the families of the internees that were arrested from Kauai, Maui, Oahu and Hawaii boarded a ship and left Hawaii from Honolulu. We and the families, except those that were later sent back to Japan on the two repatriation ships, were to spend the rest of the years together until the end of the war.

There were several individual children of the internees that were going alone to join their fathers. They were in their teens or in their twenties and could take care of themselves. Among them were two who took on the role of our spokespersons, Henry N. and Toki T., for most of the wives could not speak or understand English very well. I remember M.K., who was also there by herself, whose father had owned a Japanese bookstore.

I was seasick for four miserable days out of the five days it took to arrive in San Francisco. The ship was perhaps commissioned by the U.S. government for I thought it was not a Navy vessel for I do not recall seeing a sailor in his white uniform and cap. I went on deck a lot for some fresh air and hung on to the rails, which helped to ease the nausea. I do remember that a steward came on deck with a school bell and rang it as he shouted, "Meal time!" When I finally could romp around the deck and enjoy the sail on the last day, we sailed under the Golden Gate, more orange in color than golden, and moored in San Francisco Harbor.

We were then taken by ferry to Oakland where we got onto a Pullman train. Being a child, I was not told anything as to where we were headed. As it turned out, when we got off the train, it had taken us cross-country all the way to North Carolina in the East Coast.

As we boarded the train, I noticed that we were escorted by three FBI agents with guns and suddenly realized that I had not seen any of them since we got on the bus the day we left Hawaii until we were met by them at the Oakland train station. Maybe, they knew that all the families were anxious to meet their husbands and fathers and would not run away but to go wherever we were told to go. I am sure, escaping or running away never entered anyone's mind when we were at places unfamiliar to us and with only $250.00, how could we eat or survive. There was nothing to do but to follow orders without knowing where or what was going to happen except to know that we were being taken to meet our fathers to be repatriated together to Japan in exchange for American internees in Japan. Perhaps, the list of the people from the outer islands may have been confirmed at Fort Armstrong and then were joined by those from Oahu when we boarded the ship to depart for California. Ever since the FBI agents got on the train, they remained with us throughout our stay until we were sent to Crystal City Internment Camp in Texas in 1943.

Just before the train slowed down to stop at the Chicago station, the FBI agents told everyone to lower the window shades all the way down so that the people at the station could not see us "Japs." As far as I know, all of the three agents were polite and kind, always within our sights and never treated or spoke to us roughly and that was the only time those agents used the word "Japs" to us, perhaps to let us know that was how we were now being called by some Americans. We were also told not to peek out for if we were discovered, our train may be derailed by mobs. Curious me that I was, I could not help but crouch down and peek out when I saw a sliver of a space near the bottom of one of the two shades next to my seat. There were many soldiers in khaki uniforms with their sweethearts, wives, parents and families on the platform, waiting to go to their assigned destinations. After a while, perhaps we had stopped there for refueling, we were on our way again.

As we were crossing a long railroad bridge, one of the guards told us to look down because we were running over the famous Mississippi River. From way up high, as we looked down, I was a bit disappointed because the river looked long but we were able to see both sides of the banks and it seemed not as big and wide as I had seen in movies with large steamboats carrying passengers on them. We must have been looking at the part of the river that was narrow for we knew that the Mississippi River is large.

Being only eight years old at the time, I simply enjoyed my first train ride and was not afraid to be friendly with the guards. A.R., with his big, round eyes, strong eyebrows and middle parted black hair, B. (I did not know if it was his first or last name), with his kind face and wavy blond hair and F.S., another tall agent with a moustache wearing uniform similar to that of a police officer with a gun in a holster around his waist. A. and B. wore suits with neck ties, their guns were under the suits with shoulder holsters. They also wore hats as was the fad during those years as even Father and we used to wear hats. I still remember them as they did not seem to mind my chatting with them.

CHAPTER 4

OUR STAY, AT NORTH CAROLINA, STILL NO NEWS OF FATHER

Upon arriving at a train station in Asheville, North Carolina, we were taken by bus to the Grove Park Inn, a beautiful luxury hotel. At the time, I could not understand why we were placed there for three months, treated like hotel guests much to the chagrin of the staff. (As an adult now as I am writing this story, it occurred to me that since we were the first group of internees that were going to be repatriated to Japan in exchange for perhaps rather important Americans that were interned in Japan and were to be repatriated back to America, we were being treated carefully. Perhaps also because things were happening so quickly and maybe those in charge of these arrests were not quite prepared as to what to do with us or where to place us, we may have been sent to such a luxurious hotel as the Grove Park Inn, to give a good report back to Japan in hopes that the Americans that were interned there would be treated similarly. I have often wondered why we were sent all the way to North Carolina in the east coast and thought perhaps, to separate us from those that were arrested in the West Coast????

(Then, years later, after hearing about how those arrested in California were placed in stables and other unspeakable hardships during that time, this may be the first written story about how those of us from Hawaii were not mistreated as future repatriates in exchange for American internees in Japan as compared to the West Coast Japanese aliens and some of their American citizen children were treated as relocated enemies.)

A clerk at the front desk beckoned to me one day and shouted loudly she did not know why Japs have to be in their hotel for this was the hotel that the President of the United States stayed in when he came to Asheville. Although taken aback at her vehement exclaiming to a child and not an adult, I could only answer softly that I did not know the reason. Even knowing that we were considered enemies, it really hit home when she shouted "Japs" to me, especially since we were now on the Mainland. Hawaii makes one feel welcome and the atmosphere has what we Hawaiians call "Aloha Spirit." (However, I can now understand how she must have felt to have "enemies" stay at her hotel of which she must have been very proud to work there, being that it was The Hotel the President himself stayed at on his visits to Ashville.)

It was at the Grove Park Inn that we learned that Germans and Italians were also interned. They, too, were taken to Crystal City Internment Camp although neither they nor we tried to mingle with each other. Our mothers did not speak English, German or Italian and they did not speak Japanese so although being in the same situation, we were literally strangers with a language barrier. Since they also lived in America, they spoke English like we, the children did, but I don't remember seeing any of us talking with them. Although, those of us from Hawaii were all Japanese mothers and their children, I recall that the one German I used to see in the lobby of the hotel was a male adult. I did not see any others or their children, if they were also there at Grove Park Inn.

The rooms were cleaned by maids. We could send our dirty clothes to the laundry in pillow cases left outside our room and they would be back cleaned and pressed. Junko did the diaper laundry every day since Makoto wore them.

Meals were served to us by waiters wearing black trousers and white shirts and coats with bow ties in the dining room. I used to marvel at how they carried the big, round tray with several meals on them, held on the palm of one hand high above their shoulders.

The hotel had a wide long stairway in the back which led to a beautiful green golf course. We still have the photograph taken of the entire first group of Japanese interned from Hawaii lined up in rows on those steps.

Nearby the hotel, walking down a path toward the left was a park with many trees and a stream. In autumn, the trees were beautiful in their colors of orange and red, especially the Maple tree, which we do not have in Hawaii. The long, narrow stream nearby had several trees along one side of its shore, weeping willows with leafy branches hanging downward, pussy willow trees with tiny cotton-like buds on their branches and dogwood trees. We were warned not to wade in the stream with its clear, clean water, flowing in tiny ripples, showing some smooth rocks on its bed. It was not very deep and one could easily want to wade in the above-the-ankle, mid-shin water which seemed to beckon you to step into its cool water. We did not even try to dip our toes into the clear water because we were told of the poisonous water moccasin. Even the thought of snakes was scary and yet exciting for there are no snakes in Hawaii. Everything seemed different from Hawaii where we have no seasons.

First group of interned families from Hawaii

We, the younger children, had no physical hardships but it must have been very hard on our mothers and older children, who still did not know where our fathers were with absolutely no news of them and we had not yet been reunited with them. However, even as a child, I did realize that all of us could only follow orders that were given to us by the FBI agents, to go and do only what was allowed in those orders. After three months of such luxurious living, we were told to get ready to be moving away from there. Even without fences, barbed wires or barricades to prevent escapes, where could we possibly go and survive in a strange place where we knew we were "stamped and labeled as enemies," where hardly any Orientals are, and without funds but under surveillance of the FBI agents with guns. We were always reminded that we, too, were actually prisoners with limited freedom within that confined space.

After 3 months of such a long period of luxurious hotel lifestyle which probably most of us will never experience again, we were told to pack and be ready to move to another location. We all gathered and got onto buses and were again being taken to a destination unknown to us, wondering where we would be placed next. We did not know if we were to meet our fathers or not, still not knowing the whereabouts of them with no news or detailed information, so as usual, days to just do and follow orders without questions or answers continued.

The buses took us to Montreat, North Carolina. We stayed in a smaller, less luxurious hotel called Assembly Inn. I was always a happy and friendly child and quickly made acquaintances easily. I stopped by the front desk and chatted with Rachel and Elizabeth, the front desk clerks. They were very kind and nice to me and my siblings. They gave us candy and took photographs of us. We have photographs that Elizabeth took of us and so we are lucky to have such remembrances of the time we were there at Assembly Inn.

There again, we were guarded by the FBI agents, A., B. and F., the other agent in uniform. On some days, B also wore a similar uniform, although A always wore a suit and tie. B. was also good to the children and he must have given the model airplanes to Takaaki and his friend.

There was a lake in front of the hotel and across it on the other shore was a women's college. Students used to swim over and talk to us hanging on to the shore on our side as we stayed near them standing behind the wired fence. They always waved hello and goodbye, smiling before swimming back to their side of the lake. They were young and many of them very pretty and friendly, never making us feel like enemies or never calling us "Japs." The FBI agents stayed a distance away and only watched us but never once stopped us from chatting with the students.

Elizabeth asked me to dance a Japanese dance. After seeing me dance in my overall, she asked me to wear a kimono and dance for her. Mother used to teach us children to dance to some Japanese children's songs for the Buddhist festivals and so I wore my red kimono and sang as I danced (浜千鳥) "Hamachidori", Plover, for her. I still have the photograph from that time, although faded after being taken so many years ago. Hiromichi copied me and Elizabeth took photos of him posing with parts of the dance.

FBI Agents B. and F.   *Agent B. with Takaaki and friend*

Elizabeth, Tomoko, Hiromichi, F.M.   *Tomoko dancing "Plover*

Tomoko dancing for Elizabeth

Hiromichi dancing "Plover" and on a stone wall

We all had hats to wear as many people did then. Father wore a hat even in Hawaii before the war. Since the FBI agents, A. and B. wore hats with their suits, it must have been part of a "dressed-up" attire in those days for children.

Junko, Tomoko, Hiromichi, Norie   *Junko, Makoto*

Izumi Family, Assembly Inn

At Assembly Inn, it was everything self-service so my sister, Junko, the eldest, had to take care of us, clean the room by bringing the vacuum cleaner from wherever it was kept to do the vacuuming of our room. I don't even know where she went to do our laundry every day because Makoto was still in diapers. I do remember her carrying the ironing board and the iron to our room when she needed them to press our clothes. We always had clean clothes to wear which I took for granted. The many more hardships and responsibilities Junko had to bear and carried upon her slender shoulders compared to me, can again be attributed to our being interned. I only had to babysit my younger brothers and sisters.

Junko took all of us siblings to the dining room for our meals and we had to go along the line of people with trays to get the food served buffet-style ourselves, sat down at a table and ate there. She always took Mother's three meals upstairs to her in our room. Although she was not asked to do so, the A. family was in the room across the hall from us, and Junko also took their meals up to them since Mrs. A. had two young sons, one an infant. She would then return the dishes and trays to the dining room.

It was there, in the dining room at Assembly Inn, that I first had Macaroni and Cheese, Maple syrup for the pancakes, and Catsup, all three, which I did not like. (Since then, I still do not eat that dish or pour syrup on my pancakes. I love tomato, raw or cooked, but also discovered that I did not like catsup, even to this day.)

Hiromichi, then 6 years old, was growing pretty fast, and his shoes were getting too small for him. Mother cut the front of his shoes off and his stocking toes would be sticking out beyond the edge of the front part of the shoes. This must have hurt Mother a lot to have to do such a thing because of the amount of money she had to keep for emergencies and with the cold winter months coming. Having to do such things must have added on to the other hardships and pain she had to endure. Hiromichi, being so young and not even feeling embarrassed wearing those cut-off shoes, probably happy that his toes were not hurting anymore. I felt sorry for him and somewhat embarrassed when we went outdoors, and others could see those shoes, although no one even said a word even after they saw them. I made sure he did not go near puddles or muddy grounds so that his stocking toes would not get wet or soggy with mud.

One winter day, out of the window, we saw white flakes falling from the sky and we all dashed out to see our first snowfall. We opened our mouths and tried to eat the falling snow. Winter had set in with icicles hanging from the eaves, window sills and leaves on the trees. The coldness was something we had never experienced before; it seemed to seep into our bones like an ache. The rooms had heaters under the window sills which kept us warm but the cold outdoors was a first-time chill never felt in Hawaii.

Yarn, knitting needles and knitting instructions books were provided by the Red Cross. Junko and I knitted mittens and bonnets with long sashes that could also be wound several times around the neck like a muffler for the children. Junko was very good in making things with her hands and at thirteen years old, read the instructions and taught me what to do. I was just not good with sewing, knitting or crocheting, and was ordered by her to unravel rows of stitches and make them more even as some parts were tight and some parts were so loose, they looked like there were holes there. This was a hardship for me as I kept dropping stitches and had to unravel and do them over again so many times. I was so proud to see my younger siblings wearing the bonnets with the long sashes I had so laboriously knitted for them. Seeing the long sashes wound around their necks to keep them warm made me happy. I even knitted, with some difficulties and many unravelings, a pink vest with a cable stitch design for myself. (Junko continued to sew, crochet and knit things thereafter the war, even dresses and sweaters, caps, etc., she is very good in making handcrafted things. As for me, when I was nineteen, Mother sent me to a sewing school but after several lessons, I was asked by the principal to leave as she felt I could never master sewing. Mother always said that a girl should know how to sew for her own family and so again, when I was twenty-five, she enrolled me in her friend's sewing school but after being told many times to remove the stitches sewn so crookedly, finally when I finished sewing the one and only skirt I made, the principal told me that, even if she drew a line with a tailor's chalk, I probably could not sew straight and asked me to leave. I thought back about the time I had to knit and unravel and redo was not because I was only 9 years old but confirmed that I was just not good in small movement coordination to make things with my hands. I still find it hard to fit keys in keyholes, worse in trying to get the needle into buttonholes, drop things easily, etc.)

Winter was just around the corner when we moved to Assembly Inn and I don't recall anything special happening to us as a group during the months we spent there.

I babysat our younger siblings, played with the other children, chatted with the guards, Rachel and Elizabeth at the front desk, enjoyed chatting with the girls from the college across the lake as they came to swim on our side of the shore. I enjoyed playing in the lobby with friends when it stared to get colder outside.

Tomoko with friends in lobby

North Carolina was so different from Hawaii where we do not have really cold, icy winters. Spring was again different from Hawaii, for there, the branches on the bare trees sprouted new shoots and soon the leaves that were brown turned green. Squirrels scurried and scampered up the tree branches and disappeared into the holes in the trees, birds came back to chirp, we saw red-breasted robins, cardinals, and woodpeckers with their long, pointed beaks pecking at the trees, flowers blooming again in colorful displays.

When the weather turned warm, the coeds from across the lake swam to our shore to chat with us again.

Without realizing how the days had gone by, six months had elapsed and still we had not heard anything about our fathers, what had happened to them or where they were. The only worry that had been the most dreadful, which was whether Father was alive or not, was gone from the moment they told us that we were to join our fathers to be repatriated together with them to Japan. The loneliness and longing to be with Father never subsided for us, and I am sure the other families and children felt the same way about their fathers.

CHAPTER 5

CRYSTAL CITY INTERNMENT CAMP!
FATHER WAS THERE!

We were there at the Assembly Inn for six months when we were notified that we would be moving to Texas where our fathers were waiting for us. All of the families got on buses and again went to the railroad station to ride on a train that took us to Texas. We got off at a station near the Crystal City Internment Camp for another bus ride that took us to the camp. As we excitedly got off the buses, our fathers were waiting for us and we had a very happy reunion since our visit with them at the Kilauea Military Army Camp in Volcano, Hawaii on February 15, 1942. It was the longest one year and two and a half months of anxious insecurities, sad, lonely separation of families from Hawaii that finally ended on May 3, 1943.

Father held Mother in his arms. She was carrying Makoto, the other children were holding on to his waist, I hung on to his leg, and although we were smiling happily, tears of happiness were also shining in our eyes. Families followed their fathers to their respective homes where our internment camp lives began.

With tall, barbed wired fences surrounding the entire camp and tall towers situated at several locations, where guards with rifles watched for escapees, Crystal City Internment Camp had been built by clearing desert land. Duplex, triplex, quadriplex houses, victory huts and Quonset huts were built in different sections of the camp. The Japanese families and the German families lived in their own sections. There were three schools, a Japanese School, an English school and a German school. A market, where we could buy our daily food supplies, a small, department-store-like store that sold clothing and other necessities, purchases were bought with plastic token-like scrip used for money. The camp had a hospital with examining rooms and admission beds, a dental office in the same building. Dr. and Mrs. M. Mori, (Dr. Mori, a General Practitioner physician/surgeon, Dr. Shibuya-Mori, a pediatrician,) Dr. Furusawa, an OB-GYN specialist and another American doctor were the physicians taking care of the internees' medical treatments. The dentist was an army dental officer.

(At the last Crystal City Internment Camp reunion in Las Vegas, I met the Ichikawa siblings. Satoru, was passing out the charted drawing of the camp and gratefully gave me permission to include it in my book. This wonderfully drawn, important diagram shows exactly the high barbed-wired fences, the guard house towers, housing quarters, and locations of buildings within the enclosed "prison" where the Japanese, German and Italian internees from Hawaii, Mainland and Latin America were confined.)

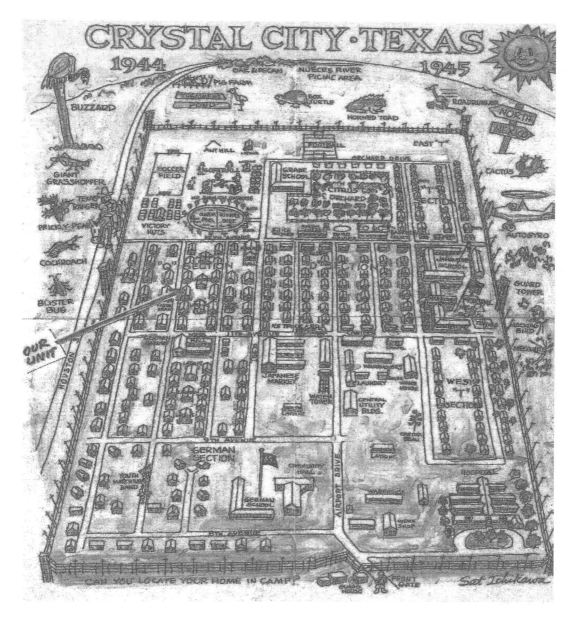

Drawn by Satoru Ichikawa, Crystal City Internment Camp

Our home, D57-A was in the duplex housing area. As we gathered around Father in our new home, he told us that he and the other detainees were sent from the Kilauea Army Military Camp to Sand Island Army Internment Camp on Oahu and then transferred to military forts on the Mainland. Father and some of the other internees were held at Angel Island, Fort McDowell in San Francisco for a short while for processing to be transferred to different military camps, (Perhaps, Father's stay there was so short, he did not mention Fort McDowell at all. This information was found out in 2015, when Mari Ito, who is like a daughter to me, was doing a research paper for her class on the second missionary of an Aiea temple who had also been arrested, found my father's name in the list of persons detained there. Some were detained for a day or a few days before they were transferred to different army forts or camps.) Father was sent to Fort Sill in Oklahoma, then, in June, 1942, he was transferred to Camp Livingston in Louisiana before settling at Crystal City in 1943 to await our arrival from North Carolina. We then told Father what we went through after the FBI took him on that dreadful night, December 7, 1941. But the joy of being able to live together was a great blessing and we could again depend on Father to be our strong pillar supporting us and not take him for granted like we used to, only realizing how much he meant to us until he was taken away from us. Our ship's Captain had been returned to us today, we had all come "home" to have him guide us. The relief and unbelievable happiness of now being able to have the comfort of being together brought forth involuntary laughter from us, just looking at Father within our sights filled the room with such joy!

The house had a kitchen, a dining/living room, 2 bedrooms, one with a bed and the other with 3 bunk beds, with a lavatory in between to be shared by the other family in the B side. It was a bit scary for the younger siblings to climb onto the upper level of the bunk bed so the older siblings slept in the upper beds. We would be eating meals cooked in our own homes and for the first time meals cooked by Mother or Father and not what was served to us without our ordering any of it. This, too, was an indescribable feeling of joy, to be able to again eat dishes we were used to eating before our internment. Perhaps, with a family as big as ours, we also had an enclosed patio in the front part of the house, which could be considered as another room. (Perhaps, the other houses also had patios but I do not recall or even remember as I did not take note of that.)

The teachers for the Japanese school, (国民学校) "Kokumin Gakko," National People's School, were the interned ministers and school teachers from various parts of the U.S., Hawaii, and Latin America. Father decided that we should attend the Japanese school as we had been told that we would be repatriated by ship to Japan.

Yoshie T., from Hawaii, was my best friend at Crystal City. She and I were the same age, enrolled in the fourth grade with other children from the Mainland as well as those from Peru. Mr. Y. (先生) "Sensei", a teacher from Peru, was our teacher.

Although we spoke English and the students from Peru spoke Spanish, during school hours, we were told to speak only Japanese. However, when we had some arguments with the students from Peru, mostly with the boys, they would shout at us in Spanish, and we shouted back at them in English. These little spats happened after school and so the teachers were unaware of them. The next day, those quarrels were forgotten and we were again friends, speaking to them in Japanese, there was no reason not to since we did not speak Spanish and they did not speak English. The reason for these spats were probably because Yoshie and I would be speaking English while walking out of the classroom after school, and they would tell us to speak Japanese. To retaliate, we used to tell the boys to speak Japanese when we also heard them speaking Spanish. Both groups would say the same thing repeatedly, shouting at each other while leaving the school grounds, they in Spanish, "Cayate la boca!," and we in English, "Shut up!" Perhaps, without realizing it, both they and we may have felt some resentment about the rule to speak only Japanese while in school, for there were periods when we got to school early before school started, or during recess or if we lingered after school to chat, since among friends, we always spoke English, and they too, must have always spoken Spanish, which may have resulted in those little spats. To both groups, once out of the classroom, we must have felt comfortable to speak in our own languages, although we were still in the hallways and not yet off the school grounds.

Although having never lived in Japan, we were repeatedly taught in school that we were children of Japan, the regimental discipline expected of us and accepted by us, may have been slowly building up unknowingly and without realizing how displeased we were at times not to voice our displeasures but to only follow and obey, may have wanted us to have those spats and to shout satisfactorily to each other in English and Spanish. Otherwise, how was it that we could make up so easily the next morning as though the quarreling had never happened and yet find ourselves quarreling again?

We simply followed what we were told to do and even to say, at times, what we were told to say. I don't remember if we repeated this every morning in school but we recited it aloud many times standing at attention beside our desks, (私は日本人です。小さいけれども、日本国民です。) "Watakushi wa Nippon jin desu. Chiisai keredomo, Nippon kokumin desu." I am Japanese. Although I am a small child, I am a Japanese citizen. Knowing that children attending Japanese school were from families that were to be repatriated to Japan, we were being taught to remember that we belonged to Japan, and that was why we were there in the internment camp. (修身) "Shushin," Morals or Ethics, was a class where we were taught the fundamental ways of a Japanese person's behavior, (忠義) "Chugi", (忠信) "Chushin" , Loyalty, (恩) "On", Obligation, gratitude towards a debt to be given back, the "On" we owe our parents are higher than mountains, deeper than oceans is a famous Japanese adage, (情) "Jou", Benevolence, Compassion, (尊敬) "Sonkei", Respect, (我慢) "Gaman," Perseverance, Patience, etc. We also learned about (大和魂) "Yamato Damashii," The Soul, Spirit of Japan, and (大和撫子) "Yamato Nadeshiko", The Spirit of an ideal Japanese women.

" Gaman!" "Gaman!" Persevere! Persevere! Father always taught us from the time we were old enough to understand that no matter how good or how bad, whatever that may happen to us, it is because the cause really lies with ourselves. We have caused it with our behavior and Karma, The Law of Cause and Effect, is one of the main teachings of Buddhism. Don't hate or contempt what is happening but "gaman" and see it through. I am sure, in order to not show any anger, bitterness and hatred for whatever hardships brought upon us from our arrests, Father and Mother endured it and did observe "GAMAN" also so that we would accept what had befallen upon us and be able to "gaman" it through. Their attitude did not erase the fact and I am sure it was the same for them and us that we were trying to "make the best" of the situation but knew that what the American government did to us was not right and inhuman.

We were being taught to be proud to be Japanese and to prepare us American citizen children, born and raised in America, to become good Japanese citizens. Who can we blame when we were being repatriated to Japan, not because we chose to go, but forced upon us? Our parents and teachers were trying to make things easier for us children to live in the war-torn country of Japan, among citizens that lived there all their lives, and in such a short time to learn why and how we would have to live among them, without shaming our family name, and to be readily accepted by them. To them, all of these practices must have been for our sakes, American citizens born and raised in a country where we lived, and were taught so many "Freedoms and Liberties." We children, not having lived in Japan, were to go to an "Old- fashioned country where children are to be seen but not heard." Now, where did I hear this expression? Mother told me this many times because I was always a chatter box. We were being trained and taught the ways of a Japanese citizen when we go to live in Japan, for most of us who had already attended English school before the war, certainly were behaving just like American children do, quite independently and outspoken, for the older teenagers, enjoying social activities like dances, get-togethers with both boys and girls mixed groups, etc. (This may have changed after the war but many schools in Japan were conducted as Boys schools and Girls schools. Mother went to an all girls' school and told me that even on the train going home, the girls sat together away from the boys and when they were teased or called by the boys, they were told by their parents to ignore them, and not even to look their way. I was told by Mother when I started my first job, if a male stranger spoke to me, to just ignore him, and walk away.)

Or, to us youngsters, being pent up and confined with rules pushed upon us, like getting up so early every morning to gather, and do the same ritual of respect to the Emperor of Japan and soldiers of the Japanese army that died in battle before the Radio exercises, especially on the cold winter months, getting up so early, may have been getting on our nerves. How nice it would have been to be able to curl up inside of a warm blanket and sleep for an hour or two more. Of course, we never complained and talked back to our parents or teachers, which was unthinkable, so we routinely did what every Japanese school student had to do. I don't know how others may have felt, but for myself, I sometimes went willingly and sometimes without showing it, unwillingly.

Every weekday morning, students of the Japanese school gathered in the courtyard of the school at 6:30 a.m., lined up in a row according to our grades and height, the tallest person in front and the shortest person in the back. One of the school teachers standing on a dais in the front of the lined up students, would lead us in verbal commands to turn diagonally to the East and (最敬礼) "Saikeirei," bow until our hands reached the level of the sides of our knees, in respect to the Emperor of Japan, then bow our heads for one minute in (黙禱) "mokutou," silent prayer, in reverence to the soldiers of Japan killed in action. We would then begin (ラジオ体操第一、 第二ラジオ体操) "Rajio Taisou Dai Ichi or Dai Ni," Radio Exercise I or II, an exercise with the teacher calling out the numbers one to eight, as we went through the routine of motions of bending our head down to where our chins touched our chest, and as far back as possible, then to the right and left, swinging our arms to the left and right, then to the front to our knees, and straight up above our heads, knee bends with hands on our waist, body bends frontward and backward. These were all motions for flexibility, also supported cardiovascular circulation, and to strengthen our muscles. I liked the mornings when "Y. Sensei," led us through these rituals. He looked so strong and fit. We were told that these same "Rajio taisou" exercises were performed throughout Japan.

We then jogged around the Japanese housing areas before coming back to the school grounds and to home to get ready for school. This was to strengthen our bodies and to be healthy children so as to not be a burden to the country when we were sent back to Japan.

Ichiko I., one of my classmates from Peru was a very smart student. She wore glasses and her hair was braided into two long, thick plaits hanging below her shoulders. She sat near me as my last name also began with I. Her penmanship was beautiful and I admired her （漢字） "Kanji," Chinese characters, which I can still see in my mind's eyes. (I always wondered what happened to her and at a Crystal City gathering we had in Honolulu, one of the ladies from Peru who went back to Japan and returned to Hawaii, told me that Ichiko had also gone back to Japan with her family post-war and that they had lived in the same neighborhood.)

Mathematics was taught in the metric system which was very different from inches, yards, miles and ounces, pints, quarts, gallons, and pounds. I had not even heard of centimeter, gram, kilogram, kilometer or liter.

Multiplication tables were easily memorized for they were taught almost like lyrics in songs. (二二が四) "Ni ni ga shi," (二三が六) "Ni san ga roku", (二四が八) "Ni shi ga hachi," (二五十) "Ni go jyu," etc.", (2x2 is 4, 2x3 is 6, 2x4 is 8, 2x5, 10, etc.) They did not go beyond the 9th table and when you learn the 3x table, you start from (三三が九) "San san ga ku", 3x3 is 9 because you have already learned that 2x3=6 so you must know that 3x2=6. When you arrive at the 9th table, you only say (九九八十一) "Ku ku hachijyuichi," 9x9, 81. They taught you that any number multiplied by 0 (zero) is Zero and any number multiplied by 1 (one) is always the same number, thus they are not included in the following tables. They start the teaching of multiplication from the 2nd table. (This method has remained in my mind and to this day, I do my multiplications in Japanese.)

Because we spoke Japanese to our parents at home and had attended Japanese School before the war, it was not difficult for me to understand or to read or write Japanese at school in the internment camp at Crystal City.

We were probably one of the families with the most children because our house had a screened patio. Father had his work desk and a chair there where he made copies of the Japanese textbooks with a blue thin paper that was laid on a slanted glass on a stand with a light bulb under it. The words were etched out with a metal pen. The etched paper was put on a (こんにゃく版) "konnyakuban," gelatin-like box hectograph, the size of the blue paper. Black ink was rubbed on that and the copies were made on the white blank paper by rolling a cylinder over it. When the entire book was copied, he folded the pages in half and punctured holes in the middle with an ice pick and sewed the pages together. I was very proud to read from the book that Father had made day after day, night after night for us.

(It was my friend, Mr. Tadashi Kanno of Tokyo, Japan, on one of his visits to Hawaii, mentioned that he attended "Kokumin Gakko" in Taiwan during the war. "Kokumin Gakko?" I was surprised to hear something so familiar, and said that I attended "Kokumin Gakko" at the Japanese school in Crystal City Internment Camp. I then asked him if he remembered the Alma Mater, (国民学校行進曲) "Kokumin Gakko Koshinkyoku". He said he did not know that there was one and he did not remember ever hearing it. I remembered the tune, but since I had not sung the song for many years, trying hard to remember the lyrics that came back to me as I sang it, were not in the correct order. As I kept singing it, I was able to put the lines that belonged to the right verse in the proper sequence. He asked me to write a short note why we were interned, and where I had learned the Alma Mater. He wanted the song written so that he could take it to his next reunion, which he was arranging. Mr. Kanno and I are the same age and he has been coordinating his Elementary School "Kokumin Gakko" classmates' reunions all these years. He also told me that I should write a story about our internment, for many people in Japan do not know the hardships suffered during the war by the Japanese aliens that had immigrated to America. When he returned to Japan, he researched and found that, in 1941, all the Japanese primary schools throughout the world, during the four years of World War II, were called "Kokumin Gakko".)

(The following information on "Kokumin Gakko" was taken "From Wikipedia, the free encyclopedia," under "Education in the Empire of Japan." I will write only the section from the period of 1937 to 1945 that pertains to "Kokumin Gakko:

"In 1941, elementary schools were renamed National People's Schools (国民学校,) Kokumin Gakko. After the start of the Pacific War in 1941, nationalistic and militaristic indoctrination were further strengthened. Textbooks such as the "Kokutai no Hongi" became required reading. The principal educational objective was teaching the traditional national political values, religion and morality. This had prevailed from the Meiji period. The Japanese state modernized organizationally, but preserved its national idiosyncrasies. Emphasis was laid on Emperor worship cult, and loyalty to the most important values of the nation, and the importance of ancient military virtues.

After the surrender of Japan in 1945, the Unites States Education Missions to Japan in1946 and again in1950 under the direction of the American occupation authorities abolished the old educational framework and established the foundation of Japan's post-war educational system.")

(I wonder how the teachers in Crystal City Internment Camp also knew about this, in order to call our school, "Kokumin Gakko.")

We sang the Alma Mater, (国民学校行進曲)" Kokumin Gakkou Koushinkyoku," Our National People's School Marching Song. I can't remember whether the 4th or the 5th verse came before the other.

(1. 今日も校舎の空高く　　御伊豆の御旗閃けば
校庭広く溌剌と　力漲る鐘の音
　　臣民我等の国民学校

　2．歴史輝く日本の　　　おいたつ誇り弁えて
学びの窓に蛍雪に　　　努力たゆまぬ幾月日
　　臣民我等の国民学校
　3．深き御恵先生の　変わらぬ慈愛父母の
真心こもるみ教えに　日ごと伸び行く友と友
　　臣民我等の国民学校

４．尊き御親の後つぎて　　国を起こさん者は誰
いざいざ共に励まして　　明日に供えぬ大覚悟
　　臣民我等の国民学校

　５．やがて御国を背負って発つ　尊き使命しっかりと
明ける亜細亜の大空へ　　　羽ばたき強く巣立つのだ
　　臣民我等の国民学校）

1. Kyou mo kousha no sora takaku
   Miizu no mihata hirameke ba
   Koutei hiroku hatsuratsu to
   Chikara minagiru kane no oto
   Mitami warera no Kokumin Gakkou

2. Rekishi kagayaku Nippon no
   Oitatsu hokori wakimae te
   Manabi no mado ni keisetsu ni
   Doryoku tayumanu iku tsukihi
   Mitami warera no Kokumin Gakkou

3. Fukaki mimegumi sensei no
   Kawaranu jiai chichi haha no
   Magokoro komoru mioshie ni
   Higoto nobiyuku tomo to tomo
   Mitami warera no Kokumin Gakkou

4. Toutoki mioya no ato tsugete
   Kuni wo okosan mono wa dare
   Izaiza tomo ni hagemashite
   Asu ni sonaeun dai kakugo
   Mitami warera no Kokumin Gakkou

5. Yagate mikuni wo seotte tatsu
   Toutoki shimei shikkari to
   Akeru Ajia no ouzora e
   habataki tsuyoku sudatsu no da
   Mitami warera no Kokumin Gakkou"

1. Today too, above our school building, the sky stands high
   As the flag of our Emperor waves unfurled
   All over the school grounds vigorously resounds
   Full of strength, the peals of the school bell
   Our National People's School
2. History brightly lights up our country of Japan
   Bringing understanding knowledge of pride for it
   Honor for the Window of Learning
   We endeavor endlessly, many months and days.
   Our National People's School

3. The deep grace and blessing of our teachers
   Are same as the love of our fathers and mothers
   Teaching us the lessons with sincerity to
   Friend and friends, as we all progress day by day
   Our National People's School

4. We will soon follow in our honorable parents' footsteps
   Who is it that will raise our country to higher goals?
   Let us start now, together as we encourage each other
   To prepare to attain tomorrow's great ambitions
   Our National People's School

5. At last the time has come for us to carry our Nation's burdens on our shoulders
   A noble mission held steadfastly strong
   To develop our goals into the frontiers under Asia's sky
   Flapping our wings powerfully forward as we fly from our nests
   Our National People's School

I still don't know the reason why Norie hated to go to the Japanese school kindergarten. (I asked her why but she also cannot remember why she did not want to go to school. Mother, from the time we were little children, whenever we misbehaved, would look up her red book of medical home remedies and give us ("灸) "yaito," moxibustion, putting a small mound of moxa and burning it. This practice was for treatments for colds and other ailments. Although punishing us, she did it with love and burned the moxa at a site where it was also a way to keep us healthy.) I only remember that on some days, Norie used get punished with "yaito" before being dragged to school by Mother.

The teachers for the English School and the Principal came from outside of the camp and taught those that wanted to finish their English requirements and graduate with diplomas. Most of the students that attended the English school were from the Mainland and some from Hawaii.

I don't remember when it was but one day, we saw some young men dressed in U.S. army khaki uniforms with khaki hats in our camp. They were soldiers of the now famed 442nd Battalion. These soldiers, having volunteered to fight in the war, had come to say goodbye to their families before being shipped out to the front. It must have been an ironic, heartbreaking moment for the parents of those soldiers, sending them off to war to fight against Japan when they themselves were imprisoned in a camp because of this war. (It was later when we found out that they were sent to the warfront in Europe to distinguish them from the Japanese army soldiers, so as to not fight against and perhaps kill brothers or relatives that lived in Japan and may have been drafted into the Japanese army. Thanks to the heroic deeds of these Japanese Nisei soldiers who fought so bravely and fearlessly, the honor and merits earned by their courageous fighting of the enemies of our country and proving their loyalty as American citizens, became the most decorated soldiers in the history of the United States with their meritorious medals. These two battalions have made all Japanese living in America much more respected and enabled them to open many doors of opportunities, which had been closed before the war. Our gratefulness and appreciation of the soldiers of the 442nd and 100 Battalions must always be remembered just as they will forever be known for their courageous valor and loyalty to our country in America's history.)

I am sorry that I have not been able to contact the composer about these two songs, or to ask for permission to write about these two songs, or to find any information about these two songs through the internet or YouTube, but they were very popular post-war. So as people will remember our courageous Nisei soldiers fighting in the European frontlines of the war, a song (I don't know its title) was written by a Japanese composer who lived in Hawaii. I heard them sung by a professional singer in Honolulu and Japan post-war. She sang it at one of the "Keirokai" shows held for the elderly members of the congregation at our Papaaloa temple after our return from Crystal City. She was originally from Laupahoehoe and visiting her family. I would like to include these songs for whenever I mention them, most people don't even know of them. Unfortunately, I remembered the melody but not the words except for a few lines of the song honoring the 442nd and 100th Battalions. I also do not know the titles to these songs.

1. （今日の来る日を知りながら）Kyo no kuru hi wo shirinagara
   （甘い二人の夢を見て）Amai futari no yume wo mite
   （明日が別れとなる夕べ）Asu ga wakare to naru yube
   　　（一目も寝ずに泣き明かす）Hitome mo nezuni naki akasu

2. （アロハの港船出する）Aloha no minato funade suru
   （恋しき人の軍服に）Koishiki hito no gunpuku ni
   　　（レイをかけるも手が震え）"Lei" wo kakeru mo te ga furue
   （涙隠した思い出）Namida kakushita omoide

3. (今イタリーかフランスか) Ima Itali kaFuransu ka
   （遠い戦地が気に掛かる）Toi senchi ga ki ni kakaru
   　　（恋しの写真抱き締め）Koishi no shashin idaki shime
   （帰ります日を泣いて待つ）Kaeri masu hi wo naite matsu

1. Knowing that this day (today) was to come
   　　But still dreaming about our sweet future
   　　On the eve that brings our parting tomorrow
   　　Unable to sleep a wink but lying awake crying

2. At the pier of Aloha where the ship will depart
   　　My beloved is wearing his army uniform
   　　Placing a lei on his uniformed shoulders
   　　With my hands trembling
   　　Left with memories of hidden tears of sorrow

3. Is he now in Italy or France?
   Worried about my beloved in the faraway battlefield
   Enfolding my beloved's photograph close to my bosom
   Crying as I await the day he will return home

Lines that are remembered as best as recalled and may not be correct, also, not in sequence of the song about our 442nd Battalion:

(共に死にたる戦友の安らかなれよ永久に)
　"Tomo ni shinitaru senyu no　yasuraka nare yo tokoshie ni"
Comrade soldier friends that together perished, may they rest in peace eternally

(ゴーフォーブロック、名も高し、四百四十二聯隊)
"Go For Broke" na mo takashi, Shihyaku shiju Nirentai"
"Go For Broke", our highly famed 442nd Two Battalions

(二世の眞、つらぬきて、世界に輝く二聯隊)
　"Nisei no makoto tsuranukite Sekai ni kagayaku Nirentai"
　Niseis of the Two Battalion's sincerity, faithfulness and loyalty penetrates and glitteringly
shines throughout the world)

As we started to live in our new environment and home, we were lucky to be in a very convenient location. The bathhouse was right next to our house and the Japanese school was right in front of the bathhouse, diagonally across from our house. Some of the houses had a toilet and wash basin but the bath houses with laundry basins were built separately here and there throughout the camp.

Upon entering the doorway of the bathhouse, which was built in a long rectangular shape, against the shorter wall were several wash basins where the laundry was done. Wash boards were furnished but the soap and scrub brush were brought by the families. Lengthwise along the building, were the shower stalls with curtains, separated by a wall in between the stalls and a long, tall wall from the ceiling to the floor in the middle of the building so that we could shower on either side of that wall. Below the up high windows on both sides so people could not see in, were long, built-in benches to put our towels and clothes on. We took our own bath soap every evening. We wore (草履,) "zoris," rubber slippers as the floor was concrete. It was scary at times for there were centipedes and scorpions found in the bath house and sometimes even in our homes.

There were unfamiliar foul smells, which we later found out were from skunks. Rattle snakes, horned toads, huge red ants that sting, black widow spiders, tarantulas were all new insects as were some poisonous reptiles that we did not have in Hawaii.

One summer day, Father, Takaaki and I were in the patio when suddenly from the ceiling, a tarantula jumped onto Father's shoulder. Takaaki, who happened to be standing behind Father, fast on his reflexes, brushed the spider off with his bare hands and when the spider hit the floor, it made a loud plopping sound.　Takaaki then grabbed ahold of the broom and with the wooden end smashed the tarantula into pieces. The tarantula was as large as a palm with black hairy legs and very venomous. Fortunately, it did not have time to sting Father but it was a frightening experience.　The tinier Black Widow spider with a red hourglass on its body was also poisonous and frightening.

The families were asked to come to the office. It must have been before August, 1944, since Katsuyo, our baby sister, born in the camp hospital, is not in the photo. A snapshot was taken of each family, perhaps, for a record of the internees that had been held in Crystal

City Internment Camp. (Since it was customary for Father to have a family portrait taken every so many years to send back to Grandmother Ko in Japan, from the time I was little, whenever a camera was brought before me, I actually posed and smiled with my head cocked and hands folded near my lap.) Junko knew that I would be smiling and posing again and so from behind me, she gruffly ordered me not to smile, that this was not a photograph that should show joy. Of course, I was already smiling widely so in haste, closed my mouth and pulled both arms to my side. The camera caught me with my mouth pulled back looking as though I was pouting. (We still laugh and make fun about my posing when we have family get-togethers if the talk turns to those days in the camp.

Izumi family, Crystal City Internment Camp

There was a hospital near the area that housed the Germans and Italians. They were in their own section of the camp and set away from the Japanese housing area. We did not play with their children since most of them must have attended the German school while most of the Japanese children went to the Japanese and English schools.

The hospital had a dental office. Dr. M. Mori, whose specialty was General Medicine and Surgery and his wife, Dr. Ishiko Shibuya, (she used her maiden name so as to not confuse the two Drs. Mori) Pediatrician, treated the patients in the two examination rooms. Although there was an American doctor also, I did not see him throughout our stay at the camp.

37

The dentist was an U.S. Army dentist dressed in Khaki uniform. The dental clinic was across the medical clinic on the right side of the entrance to the hospital as you enter it.

Dr. F., an OB/GYN specialist, and his wife lived in the other unit of our duplex home, D 57-B. Dr. F. and Mother walked to the hospital together when she gave birth to our sister, Katsuyo, on August 18, 1944. That was the only birthing that Mother had a doctor attending her. (Among the 12 children's birthings, the babies were born before the doctor could come to the delivery room. She always had the babies in the early hours of the morning and although admitted in a hospital, by the time the doctors arrived from their homes, she had already given birth.) I suggested giving an English name, Crystal, to the newborn sister, but Father opposed the idea and named her Katsuyo (with the "Kanji" characters, ("勝,) "Katsu," to win and (世,) "Yo," world. Perhaps, he chose those characters that way, hoping that she would excel in her life or maybe wishing for Japan to win the war and to free us from the camp. Of course, Father refusing to give Katsuyo an English name was understandable under the circumstances we were in, but I simply thought Crystal would be an appropriate name since she was born in Crystal City and had no other thoughts and so did not feel hurt that he refused my suggestion and also because none of us had English names. Junko, after school, always gave Katsuyo a bath before doing the other chores.

I had a terrible experience when I went to the dentist because my two front teeth were aching. The dentist did not explain or say anything to me and started to drill the backs of the teeth. It was much later that I found out that he simply drilled it and killed the nerves. I was 10 years old at that time but I cried out in pain and nearly jumped off the chair for he did not give me anything to numb the area. Gaby, the dental assistance, was a very pretty German girl internee and she comforted and soothed me. She gave me a photo of herself as we became friends. (I am sorry I could not find her photo, which I would have wanted to put in this book. After a few years, the teeth turned gray and I could not smile widely because I felt embarrassed. When we moved to Honolulu, gratefully, Dr. M. U., a member of the congregation, kindly offered to pull them out and made a bridge in its place. I was very happy and went right back to smiling with my front teeth showing.)

Since the Izumi family lived in the first row of the duplex houses across from the Japanese school, after the early morning rituals and the Radio exercises, I and my siblings could reach home by just crossing the road to get ready for school. Students that lived quite a distance away from the school ground had to hurry home, eat breakfast, get ready for another school day and walk back to the school before it started.

The weather was very hot, sometimes up in the 100+ degrees during summer and very cold in the winter. It snowed briefly one winter but the snow melted as soon as it touched the ground. The thunder and lightning storms were unlike any we had in Hawaii. Lightning flashing and brightening the sky, almost like a brief daylight, loud claps of thunder, raindrops drumming loudly, incessantly down on the corrugated sheet metal roof in unstopping beats, were frightening. Sleet, sudden hail storms, made us run to find shelter by holding the swings over our heads to protect us from the pelting. Icicles on eaves and window sills were weather conditions we had never experienced before in Hawaii.

There was a set of swings in the Japanese part of the camp and we used to go there to ride them. One day, as I stood in line to await my turn, a little German girl and her father stood behind me. It was the first time a German child had come when I was there. When it was my turn, I turned around and told her father that she could ride the swing before me. He smiled, patted me on my head and said what sounded like, "Shoenes kind", which I thought meant "Nice child." That was the only time I saw a German family on our side of the camp. I hardly saw any German children because, just as I did not go to where they were housed, they probably also did not come to the Japanese housing area of the camp. The boys that delivered the ice looked like they were Germans but rushing to deliver the block of ice before they melted, we did not even chat with them.

When standing before it and facing our house, on the left side were families from Hawaii and some from the Mainland. The Rev. Y. of the Tenri-kyo sect was from the Mainland and his daughter, I., was a new friend. From Hawaii were the Rev. M.'s family, the M.s, the Rev. Miyamoto family, whose daughter, K., I played with. She had older siblings, brother, Clifford Terufumi and sister T. (Our Crystal City reunions in Honolulu will be thankfully headed and arranged by her brother, Clifford T., who has held us together even to this day, to remember those years of confinement and to renew our friendships made there during that time.)

Crystal City Internment Camp luncheons. Clifford seated, left

On the other half of the Miyamoto's duplex was the Fukuda family, and the English School was across the road from their homes. Further on where the road turned to the right were the Okazaki family and the I. family. Those two families were from the Mainland.

The Fukuda family had 3 daughters, Fumiko, Yukiko and Yayoi. Their father was my 5th and 6th grade teacher. Mrs. Fukuda and Mother became very good friends almost from the time they met and Yayoi and Junko became good friends also. (Mother and Junko continued their friendships with them after we moved to Honolulu.)

The road turned right and in the corner lived the Okazaki. family and the I. family from California. I used to go to the Okazaki house with Toki, who was friends with Maru. (After moving to Honolulu, I found Toki working at a jewelry store office in the Ala Moana Shopping Center. I went to visit her often and she always smilingly came out of the office into the store to chat with me.)

I went to learn calligraphy, (書道,) "Shodou,") penmanship with (筆,) "fude,") brush and (炭,) "sumi," charcoal ink from Rev. I., a (日蓮宗,) Nishiren Shu,") Nichiren sect minister. Rubbing the charcoal stick with water in the rectangular stone-like dish had a specific way of doing it, like writing the (ひらがな,) "hiragana," Japanese alphabet character (の,) "no," pronounced no. His eldest daughter, T., was a new friend from California.

I used to go to chat with Tayeko Ogawa, Nancy Kawashima and Ruby and Betty Fukunaga, at their homes, new friends I made from California. Later on when some families from Tule Lake moved to Crystal City, I walked to the Victory hut area and chatted with Masako and Yukio, the O. siblings and new classmates.

The boys and young men from Tule Lake had their hair clipped down to their scalp or either buzzed off with the (バリカン,) "barikan," hair clippers, like boys in Japan (bald headed) and even their baseball team was called "Nippon." They seemed to have much stronger feelings about being Japanese.

The T.s and T.s, families from Hawaii, lived in the triplex housing area and because it was near a grove of orange trees, we referred to that area as (オレンジ村,) "Orenji Mura," Orange Village.

Hiromichi and I used to go there together, for Mother always sent me with Hiromichi when he went to play with Akiyoshi T., son of Rev. T. from Hawaii.

Mother with Mrs. Fukuda at Assembly Inn

There was an auditorium where the first rows of quadriplex houses were built and we went to Sunday school there. Whenever all of the different Buddhist sects' members congregated for the Festival services celebrating花祭,) "Hanamatsuri,) Wesak Day when Shakamuni Buddha was born and (浄土曽,) "Jodo-E," Bodhi Day when Shakamuni Buddha became Enlightened, Rev. F. from the Jodo Mission chanted the (四弘誓願,)"Shiguzeigan," a Buddhist gatha (hymn) and girls from his sect, dressed in pink flowing robes with gold-colored tiaras, danced with beating the rhythm on the (鼓,) "tsuzumi," hand drum and tossing red and pink paper petals to the floor from gold-colored dishes with ribbons streaming downward from them. (Later, after returning to Hawaii, Rev. Miyamoto and Rev. F. will become bishops of their Jodo Mission temples in Hawaii.)

There was an icebox without electric power in every home and a block of ice was delivered by two Caucasian young boys (German high school boys?) One would be driving the truck with a tarpaulin sheet covering the ice in the back of the truck. The other boy, wearing gloves, would use an ice pick along the lines on the ice, which broke it off into the exact size that fit into the upper part of the icebox, which was the freezer. He would carry the ice with two handles that opened wide into two large prong-like hooks, grasped the block of ice and placed it into the top compartment of the ice box. Milk was also delivered to the homes in bottles, with thick cream on the top. We shook the milk until the cream merged with the milk before we drank it. It was very rich and rather sweet. The ice and the milk were two things that we never ran out of for they were always delivered to us. Marketing was done often so that the meats, fruits and vegetables that were perishable could remain fresh. Probably, the icebox was not as cold as an electrically run one but nothing spoiled in it.

Marketing was done with rationing, by the number of persons in a family, and numerical plastic scrips that looked like tokens were used in place of money. We had a two-wheel box-like wooden cart as did the other families there. We used to put our groceries in it whenever we went to the market, also when we went shopping at the store that sold clothing and other merchandises. In our family, Father did all the shopping and at times, some of us would go along with him. I looked forward to the days when I could go shopping with him.

Some families planted vegetables in the back of their house. Almost every house with a garden planted watermelon. We also had green onion, eggplant, string beans, carrots and pumpkin in our backyard.

Father used to cook for us occasionally and one of my favorite dishes was pork and ginger cooked in （味噌,） "miso," bean paste, brown sugar, (醤油,) "shoyu," soy sauce and vinegar. He added small-sized onions whole and (大根,) "daikon," long radish cut round in it. By using pork belly, the fat in between the lean portions made it soft and melted in the mouth. I also loved the beef soup he made with onion, carrot, celery and especially, the okra he put in it. I still remember that Norie did not like the okra, which I loved. Okra and eggplant are two of my favorite vegetables.

One day, Father came home with an ice cream machine. He put the mixture of milk, sugar, eggs and vanilla in the container which had a handle that connected with the churner in the middle of it and protruded outside of the bucket. This handle had to be turned manually so that the churner in the bucket would stir the mixture. Father put ice chips and salt around the container in the bucket, adding more ice and salt as he turned the handle. We waited eagerly as the turning of the handle became more difficult and finally, the ice cream had hardened so the handle became stuck. We enjoyed the home-made ice cream and had to eat it all since the ice box had no freezer.

Junko baked a lemon meringue pie from a recipe that was on the outside of the Corn Starch box. It was the first time I ate it and loved it. (Lemon Meringue Pie is still my favorite pie.) Mother even made cream puffs for us which was a delightful surprise for although she was a good cook, she had never baked any pastries before. We wanted to eat (いなり寿司,)

"Inari sushi," cone sushi and because (油揚げ,) "aburaage," fried tofu, which was not available at the time, she made the cone out of flour, salt and water. After the years of not eating sushi, it was delicious and wonderful. I think, perhaps, the meaning of "Necessity is the mother of invention" may not apply here but we experienced a lot of things differently from before by improvising and using what was available during our internment.

"Tofu" was sold at the market but it was not tasty, however, Japanese people all love "tofu" and it sold out very quickly and never enough to go around. What is "Miso" soup without "tofu," what is "Sukiyaki" without "tofu," fresh raw "tofu" is delicious with soy sauce and grated ginger or radish, fried "tofu" by itself is another delicious dish, mashed "tofu" used in "Shiraai" with Won Bok or water cress is a great side dish, oh, so many Japanese menus call for this delicious ingredient that many of us may not be able to imagine what it would be like without "tofu." Bishop Fujii went to speak to the Administrator of the camp and asked to have a "tofu factory" in the camp where some ladies could make "tofu," which was very much in demand by many families. Permission was granted and in one of the victory huts, a "tofu" factory where production of enough of this delicious "Japanesey food, "tofu" was made. It was a joy to be able to go to the market at any time to buy "tofu" and find it always available.

(I love "tofu" and when we lived in Guam for nearly two years from early 1964, there were no Japanese restaurants and no direct flights from Japan to Guam. During my two pregnancies, I had no morning sickness but missed eating "tofu" since it was not available. After we left Guam, we went to visit my husband's family in Hong Kong and no sooner did I step into the doorway where his mother lived and was waiting for us to arrive, I held her hand and said, "Mommy, tofu." I had no idea I was going to say that, it just popped out of me the moment I saw her kind face. She looked at me, pregnant 7 months, and said, "Poor girl." Promptly, she went to the wall telephone and made a call. A few minutes later, a delicious "tofu" dish was delivered to her home from a Chinese restaurant. I was so surprised and immediately was so happy to be in Hong Kong and thought that it was a wonderful place, so convenient and service at your fingertips.)

Boy Scouts and Girl Scouts were organized with Scout Master T. and Girl Scout Leader, Dr. Ishiko Mori.

Both scout troops had their own flags. The boy scouts wore khaki uniforms with neckerchiefs and hats. Our flag, white with a red plum blossom in the center and uniforms were designed by Dr. Mori. We had summer uniforms, white short-sleeved dresses with a green neckerchief and in winter, long-sleeved khaki dresses with the same green neckerchief.

Boy Scout leaders with neckties, scouts with neckerchiefs

Boy Scout Leaders with their flag

Girl Scout Leader, Dr. Ishiko Mori

Girl Scouts in Khaki and white uniforms with flag and some mothers

The girl scout troops were divided into age levels or the school grades so again, Yoshie T., Tomoko Takeuchi and I were in the same Troop 3. Each troop had an older scout as their leader and ours was Caroline S. Fujisawa. (Our link of friendship must be very strong, for after moving to Honolulu to this present day, Caroline and I seem to coincidentally meet while shopping and at different places, and of course, at our Crystal City reunions arranged by Clifford Miyamoto. Her father was also a Buddhist minister. The older scouts that led the different troops wore a white blouse, Khaki suit with a green handkerchief in the suit pocket during winter.

Girl Scout Troop 3 with Leader, Carolyn Fujisawa in summer uniform. Yoshie T, second from left last row, Tomoko Takeuchi on extreme left second row, Tomoko Izumi on extreme right front row.

Dr. Mori was a poet and she wrote lyrics to, (少女団の歌,) "Shojodan no Uta," (Girl Scouts Song,) which we sang to the tune of one of her favorite songs.

少女団の歌

１．　此処テキサスの砂漠にもユーカリの花の香りあり
　　　苦痛しく移し植えられて　我等は大和撫子よ　　　　　同じ親より咲き出でぬ

２．　清き心の純潔は散りおもいとい胸深く
　　　若き血潮の紅は鬼をも泣かす情けあり
　　　大和乙女を君知るや

46

３． 朝日に匂う桜ぞと兄のたまえば我も又
　　雪中に咲く紅梅と答え祭りて微笑みつ
　　テキサス嵐吹かば吹け

４． 大和臣民の誇りなる正義と愛を身に締めて
　　世界の果てに隔つとも良き乙女どち手を取りて
　　共に理想の月を見ん）

1. 　Koko Tekisasu no sabaku nimo
　　Yu-kari no hana no kaori ari
　　Kutsushiku utsushi uerarete
　　Warera wa Yamato nadeshiko yo Onaji oya yori, saki idenu

　2. 　Kiyoki kokoro no junketsu wa Chiriomo itoi mune fukaku
　　Wakaki chishio no kurenai wa Oni omo nakasu nasake ari
　　Yamato otome wo kimi shiruya

　3. 　Asahi ni niou sakura zoto Ani no tama eba ware mo mata
　　Secchu ni saku koubai to Kotae matsurite hohoe mitsu
　　Tekisasu arashi fukaba fuke

　4. 　Yamato mitami no hokori naru Seigi to ai wo mi ni shimete
　　Sekai no hate ni hedatsu tomo
　　Yoki otome dochi te wo torite
　　Tomo ni risou no tsuki wo miun

1. 　Here, also in the desert of Texas
　　Is the fragrance off Eucalyptus flowers
　　Through our hardship and pain, transplanted here
　　We, the ideal maidens of Yamato (Japan as called in the days of yore) From the same
　　　　　　parents, blooming forth

2. Pure hearts of these maidens, scatter in regret,
　　However, in their loving hearts, deep
　　Their young blood, crimson, can also make
　　Even the Devil cry with their compassion
　　Be aware of the spirit of a maiden of Yamato

3. In the morning sun, the scent of the Sakura
　　If my brother is a gem, so am I
　　Even as I bloom as a red plum blossom in the snow
　　I smile in response to my dedication
　　Storms of Texas, blow, and blow more as you will

4. We are the people of proud Yamato (Japan)
   With honesty and love wholeheartedly
   To the ends of the earth, we will go forth
   We, good maidens, hand in hand
   Together, with our ideal goals, dreams and hopes
   Gazing at the moon

The boy scouts and girl scouts met in the grounds behind the English school and we marched to drill commands called out as they were in the Japanese military army. (It was similar to drills marched by soldiers, with commands like, "Attention! Forward march! About face! etc.," but ordered in Japanese. This too, was to exercise and keep healthy. It was at these scout gatherings that we students from Hawaii and Peru that attended Japanese school were able to mix with the students that went to English school and become friends.

Movies were shown in the area that was flat and open with a sheet that was hung on the wall of a building for a screen. We used to take our chairs to sit and watch the movies. Whenever there was to be a sumo match, a (土俵,)"dohyou," the sumo ring was made there too.

Every evening, the men would carry their folding chairs and gather to hear the news of the day there. Bishop F., who spoke English and was the designated spokeman for the Japanese, would go to the Camp Director's office and listen to the news in English on the radio and announce it to them in Japanese.

To celebrate the Japanese festivals and holidays, dates like the birthdays of the Emperors of Japan, (雛祭,) "Hina Matsuri," Girl's Day Dolls Festival, (演芸会,) "Engei Kai," stage shows were held in the English school auditorium. (演歌,) "Enka," Songs of Japan sung by the O. sisters, M. and S., (舞踊,) "Buyo," Japanese dance danced by K.S., Tomoko Takeuchi and K.T. Tomoko's father, Bokuhei Takeuchi, sang （義太夫節,）" Gidayu-bushi," a form of song sung in a narrative style at （文楽,）"Bunraku," puppet shows, accompanied by Mrs. M. on the （三味線、）"Shamisen," 3 stringed Japanese banjo. Hawaiian hula dances by C.M., (芝居,) "Shibai," play, drama acted out about famous stories. Everyone showed up to watch these shows.

When the Girl's Day Festival was celebrated for the first time, Dr. Mori decided that the stage setting would be the "Hinamatsuri" (Dolls Festival) display dolls and chose girls from the scout troops to sit on the wide steps prop built. I was chosen as the first (お雛様,) "Ohina-sama," Empress doll, K.N. as the (お内裏様,) "Odairi-sama," Emperor doll and we sat on the top level of the wide step-like stairs. My friends, Yoshie T. was the (右大臣,) "U Daijin,") Minister of the Right, Tomoko Takeuchi was also the middle doll on the second step just below me, as one of the （三人管女、）" Sannin Kanjo," three court ladies, and Tayeko Ogawa was the extreme right doll as one of the three （仕,）（衛士,）" shi," "Eishi," guards on the first step. There were four steps and each step had the girls portraying the dolls that are displayed on that row of steps like they are on Dolls Day. We were dressed like the dolls in each role and were ordered not to move, talk to each other or even smile as we were supposed to be dolls. This was a bit difficult for me, dressed as an Empress wearing a crown that had trinkets hanging down from it, sitting at the very top and trying to watch the show below. Father told me later that he was worried I might fall from the top step since it was quite high up. We had to watch the backs of the singers and actors as we were the background decoration prop. After the show, a photograph was taken with some scouts. The little girl with curly hair on the right of the "Sannin Kanjo" is Itsu Takeuchi, Tomoko's sister.)

Girl scouts Hinamatsuri dolls and other scouts after the show

From the beginning of our meeting, M.O., also from Hakalau on the Big Island, treated me like her little sister.

M.O. (left) with her siblings

M. and her younger sister, S. always sang at every show but strangely, I don't even remember any of the songs sung by S. At one of these shows, M. sang a song about a fat round baby as he grows into youth, then an adult which I still remember just from listening to her practicing it at her home before the event. It was titled, (丸東平,) "Maru Touhei," Round Eastern Soldier and was probably written during the Japan-China War.

（１．僕は丸々丸東平　丸々部隊の人気者
　　今は丸々方面で　丸々任務にご奉公

　２．さん丸丸月丸日に　丸々陣の戦いで
　　敵の丸々丸々隊　分捕りしたのも僕の隊

　３．僕が生まれた其の時も　丸々太った桃太郎
　　産湯の盥も真ん丸で　デンデン太鼓も丸かった

　４．小学校では宿題も　　何時も丸々二重丸
　　木登りゴッコで落っこちて　　瘤まで丸いと笑われた

　５．青年団の競技でも　徳意は丸い砲丸だ
　　村の相撲じゃ横綱で　丸い土俵の花形だ

　６．今は戦地の鉄兜　　丸い月影夜が明ける
　　進軍ラッパに朝の風　仰ぐ国旗も日の丸だ）

1. Boku wa maru maru maru touhei,
Maru maru butai no ninki mono
Ima wa maru maru houmen de
Maru maru ninmu ni gohoukou

2. San maru, maru getsu, maru nichi ni
Maru maru jin no tatakai de
Teki no maru maru maru maru dai
Bundori shita no mo boku no tai

3. Boku ga umareta sono toki wa
Maru maru futotta Momotaro
Ubuyu no tarai mo manmaru de
Denden daiko mo maru katta

4. Shougakkou dewa shukudai mo
Itsumo maru maru nijuu maru
Kinobori gokko de okkochite
Kobu made marui to warawareta

5. Seinen dan no kyougi demo
Tokui wa marui hougan da
Mura no sumo ja Yokozuna de
Marui dohyou no hanagata da

6. Ima wa senchi no tetsu kabuto
Marui tsuki kage yo ga akeru
Shingun rappa ni asa no kaze
Aogu kokki mo Hinomaru da"

In this song the word "Maru" means at times something secretive and at times, round in shape.

1. I am a maru maru maru (round) soldier,
the most popular one in this maru maru (secret) battalion
I am now stationed at a maru, maru (secret) location,
Serving in a maru maru (secret) mission.

2. On a maru maru month, on a maru maru day,
we attacked a maru maru battle camp.
The enemy's maru maru squadron,
It was my maru maru squadron that captured them.

3. When I was born, I was a fat maru maru Momotaro.
 (Peachboy from a Japanese fairy tale)
My wash basin was perfectly round
And even my tummy was also round.

4. For my elementary school home work,
I always got round 2 circles (In those days,
Japanese school grades were marked by red-colored circles)
 I fell off while playing climbing a tree.
Everyone laughed to see that even the lump
from the bump was round.

5. At the Young Men Association sports events
My pride and confidence was in the shot-put game.
At the village Sumo competition as a Yokozuna、
I was the champion of the round "dohyo" (round Sumo Ring).

6. I am now wearing a helmet at the war front
The moon's round shadow tells of the evening's end into the start of nightfall.
Sounds of tap from the round bugle signaling
forward attack in the morning breeze.
Even the flag of the country I salute is the ("Hinomaru")
the round rising sun pennant of Japan.

One day when I was playing at M.'s home, she washed and curled my hair with a hot curling iron. I was thrilled to have curly hair and hurried home to show it to my siblings. Father saw me first and instead of saying I looked nice, to my dismay, he promptly carried me to the sink and washed the curls out saying that Japanese girls do not have curly hair. (Unless Japanese girls were born with naturally curly hair, they wore their hair like the Japanese dolls with bangs and straight hair of different lengths unlike the Caucasian girls, many who had naturally curly hair. Besides, this may have been to remind me that I was Japanese, although also an American citizen. He was displeased with my curly hair, but I sort of understood how he felt, for he did not say what he did harshly and gently wiped my hair dry.

I probably met Aya H. from Girl Scouts since she attended English school and she also treated me like a little sister. One day I went to meet Aya at the English school. She and the other girls from the high school classes had gathered at a room there and were cutting crepe paper to decorate the auditorium for a dance. They were all excited about being able to have a prom in the camp just like all English schools outside have dances in high schools. Aya was also drawing a poster. She was a beautiful girl with a talent for drawing. She told me to sit down and to look at the magazines that were there. There was a magazine called Modern Screen that had photos of the movie stars of the time and showed pictures of some scenes from the movies. It was the first time I had seen a movie magazine. I thought perhaps a teacher may have brought it in for the students. Aya gave me a photo of herself, which I treasured. (I could not find the album I had pasted it in after returning to Hawaii among the many albums we have, so asked Clifford Miyamoto to give me a copy of her photo from his school annual. She was the Campus queen and the most popular girl, which I found out from the annual. That made me very happy and proud of her. She did not even tell me about this or boast about her popularity.) I liked looking at Aya and just being with her made me feel nice and happy. Students that attended the English school had photographs taken for their annuals and other events but those of us who attended Japanese school do not have any school photographs. (I don't remember Japanese school having special events, thus perhaps, no photographs were taken. I wonder if during those years, if those that attended Japanese school there had a graduating class and if photographs were taken.)

Aya H., Campus Queen, the most popular girl

There was a time when I had difficulty reading a book or seeing things that were close. My vision was fine when looking at things in the distance but blurry when things were near. I told Dr. Mori about this and arrangements were made for me to have my eyes tested. It was exciting for I went with a soldier in an olive green automobile to San Antonio and had my eyesight checked. At 11 years old, I was diagnosed with far-sightedness which is really rare for someone my age. A few days later, I was given a light-colored coral, plastic framed glasses, which I wore when studying or reading. The glasses must have been from army supply stock because the army dentist wore glasses with the same kind of frame. After several months, the words became blurry with the glasses on, and just as suddenly as I became far-sighted, I was suddenly back to normal vision. At least, this incident gave me a ride out of the barbed-wire fences in my first automobile ride since we left Hawaii.

It was very hot during the summer and permission was given for the men to dig a swimming pool. An Italian engineer internee designed the pool and fathers and young men, Japanese, Germans and Italians together dug out the dirt. After several weeks of doing labor he was not used to, Father complained of low back and leg pain. He was diagnosed with neuritis. The pool was finished with concrete. There was the shallow side with a rope line spanning the middle to indicate that beyond that line was the deep end of the pool. We were warned that the deep side was quite deep. I remember that it was round, very big and many people could swim in it at the same time, which many of us enjoyed, especially on those hot, hot days. It was the best and most enjoyable pastime, for there would be so many of us at the pool. Perhaps swimming at the pool was the most times we mingled with the Germans and Italians, although I did not make any new friends among them. Because it was also wide, for the younger children, we could swim, wade or just sit in the width of the shallow side instead of swimming toward the line that divided the deep side and the shallow side of the pool.

(Today, most everyone who stay in the sun for a swim, picnic or hikes, etc., for any number of hours, rubs on sunscreen cream to prevent skin cancer but in those days, the word cancer was not even mentioned and perhaps, not even diagnosed yet as a disease. It may have been known to the medical world, but it could be that, as a child, I was not interested to know or except to know diseases other than the cold, appendicitis, tonsillitis, and the childrens' communicable diseases such as measles, chicken pox, mumps, etc. I don't know if sunscreen creams were even sold then but I did not know about them.)

Father had befriended Mr. T. while digging the pool. Like Father, Mr. T. was also originally from Hiroshima. Mr. T. came to our home to give Father (指圧,) "shiatsu,)" finger-pressure therapy for his low back and leg pain neuritis from the weeks of digging the pool. One of the times when he was over, I had a cold and Mr. T. gave me a massage and said that by squeezing the muscles on top of the shoulders from the end of the neck towards the arms can improve the condition and also prevent colds. It was very painful but it worked, for the following day, I was well. He helped with starting our vegetable garden and oversaw it whenever he visited Father. (I may be mistaken about this, but I recall that Mr. T. had two daughters that were in the Girl Scouts, M. and R.)

It was a very hot summer day when I asked Mother if I could go swimming. Since Junko was not able to take me, she did not allow me to go. Knowing that Mother did not allow back taIk, I started to softly whine and muttered under my breath how hot I felt several times. Without a word, Mother brought out the haircut scissors and cut my below-the-shoulder length hair to above my ears and said that I should now feel cooler. Needless to say, I was very sad and regretful to have my hair cut short like a boy's, but certainly learned my lesson the hard way. Perhaps she did this so harshly because, sadly and shockingly, two girls from Peru that were close friends with each other had recently drowned in the pool. We were all very sad for we knew them, as they were girl scouts in a younger troop than ours. (This incident of my shortened haircut is laughingly told at the family gatherings and even the younger children knew that I was quite self-willed and a rascal in my childhood.)

Father loved to write (短歌,) "Tanka," Japanese poem of 31 syllables and wrote them for years. Dr. and Mrs. Mori also were poets. They joined more than 30 other persons and formed a Tanka club. I don't remember how many times they met and wrote poetry together. They did put together a book of poems called (流れ星,) "Nagare Boshi," Shooting Star. The drawing on the cover was done by a member of this poetry club. We saw shooting stars quite frequently in the clear night sky. Somehow, in Texas, the stars seemed bigger and shone so brightly.

Nagare Boshi cover

I went to play many times at the home of the Drs. Mori. They treated me like their own daughter for their children did not come to the camp. (Even after the war, when the Izumi family moved to Honolulu in 1951, they continued to pick me up and take me to their home and I spent many happy times with them. Mrs. Mori made the most delicious miso soup with shaved dried bonito flakes. She would order (握り寿司,) "Nigiri Sushi," from (京屋,) "Kyo-Ya," which was the best Japanese restaurant in those days. Dr. Mori used to like for me to massage his legs. He told me to always rub the leg from down to upward and never downward.)

(Dr. Mori had his clinic on Nuuanu Avenue and he became our primary physician. I was 17 years old when we moved to Honolulu and both Drs. Mori were happy to see me again. I was very thin at 89 pounds and also anemic and suffered fainting spells, although infrequently. Dr. Mori treated me with a shot once every week and was delighted when I started to gain even a pound. I fluctuated between 89 and 91 pounds but he treated me until I recovered from my anemic condition.)

Coming back to our camp days, I went to see Dr. Mori at the hospital because I found an ugly wart to the right of the mid top of my lip. It was skinny and longish rather than flat. He pulled a single strand of hair from my head and tied the wart tightly with it at the bottom. He said that since there would be no circulation there, the wart will die and drop off. Several days later, without my knowing when, the strand of hair and the wart were gone. It was indeed a very painless treatment.

Yoshie T. and I became friends as soon as we met on the boat from Hawaii to California. Our families became friends, her father was a minister of the same sect, "Jodo Shinshu," as Father and our mothers became friends. Each child in their family had a friend in four siblings from our family. They had a baby sister born in the Crystal City hospital just like our sister was born there also. When I went over to their house to play, I used to see her father carving Buddhist images and other objects out of wood. He was very artistic and so was Yoshie. She was tall and I was short so although we were in the same grade at school and in the same troop at Girl Scouts, she was always either the first in line or the last and I was always the last or the first in line.

Nancy Kawashima, a new friend from California, had a birthday party at her home and I wanted to have Father help me buy her a gift. Instead of taking me to the shop where we used to buy clothing and other merchandise, he wrapped three large cans of Del Monte peaches in newspaper and told me to give that as a present. I was unhappy and embarrassed about such a gift but he assured me that her family would enjoy them. We had a large family and so we were able to buy more than other families since produces and other food products were allotted by rationing according to the number of people in a family. Grudgingly, I took the peaches and to my surprise, Nancy's mother was delighted with the gift. However, I still felt it was not a gift that Nancy, a child, would enjoy. (This incident somehow left a lingering impression for I, still at my elderly age, do not like canned peaches.)

(Now, remembering in retrospect, I am certain that our parents and the older siblings had to endure many hardships but as an 8-year old child, I enjoyed the train ride, the beautiful Grove Park Inn, even the self-serving Assembly Inn, and the many friends I made from Hawaii, Mainland and Peru. I became friends with 3 girls with the name, Tomoko, 2 were from Hawaii and Tomoko Takeuchi from California. Although I did not have the opportunity to become friends with her, I knew that one of the twins in the Girl Scouts was also a Tomoko. So, as far as I can remember, there were five of us with the same first name of Tomoko in Crystal City. Of course, perhaps there may have been others with that name, but I did not know them. (At the last reunion held in October, 2015 at Las Vegas, I met Tomoko Uzuhashi Mizukami from California. She was a friendly, cheerful person with a ready smile and we felt the closeness of having the same name. At that moment, I decided that I would include her as a new friend and another "Tomoko" who was in the internment camp with us.)

The days went by rather routinely, I don't recall being afraid of being kept within barbed wires and watched by guards with rifles. I don't know of any tragic incidents occurring due to anyone trying to escape and to my recollection, we were pretty much left alone to do whatever we wanted to within those high barbed-wired fences. From the time the war began when Father was arrested and when we left Hawaii to join Father, to when it ended and left the camp, during those years, I made many new friends that were in Crystal City Internment Camp with us.

One day, a man from Bolivia and his little son, came to visit us and said that he was Father's cousin, KantaroTakamori, from his mother's side of the family. Father, having lost his mother when he was five years old, did not remember her parents or know any of his mother's relatives. Takamori had heard about his cousin, Kakusho Izumi, before he immigrated to Bolivia so he knew about Father. It is almost eerie, even ironical that they should finally meet at the Crystal City Internment Camp in Texas because of the war and their being interned. Father was very happy to meet him. His cousin had emigrated to Latin America, settling in Bolivia and married a woman from there but she had not come to the camp with them. He was an artist and asked Father for a loan of money. (I don't know if the loan was made with the scrip tokens or with American dollars, if we had any left, which was not usable in the camp anyway.)

He said that he could not return this loan and that he would like to draw a portrait in return. Father had a photograph of his mentor and beloved teacher, "Bishop (是山恵覚、)"Koreyama Ekaku." He asked for a portrait of his teacher and because our cousin did not have any oil paints, water color paints or brushes, the portrait was done in pencil and perhaps, charcoal. It turned out so realistically drawn that father was very happy and satisfied. He always hung it on his bedroom wall above his bed.

(Whenever we moved into a new home until the day he died, he always hung the portrait on his bedroom wall above his bed, praying and thanking the Bishop after his daily morning and evening (お参り,) "omairi," prayer before the Buddhist altar.) We, the children, were fascinated and sometimes felt weird because wherever we moved to and fro in front of the portrait, it seemed as though the Bishop's eyes followed us.

Photo and portrait of Bishop Ekaku Koreyama

Two ships had sailed with families from Hawaii, Mainland and Latin America, just as we were told, to be repatriated and sent back to Japan, to be exchanged with the Americans that had been interned in Japan. I did not even know which of my friends' families had gone on those ships. Twice, our name had not been on the repatriation list and Father made an inquiry to the Spanish Embassy since Spain was in a neutral position in this war. No reply or explanation was given for the reason why we were not included in those repatriations. As it turned out, we were fortunate to have been excluded from the lists.

(It was several years after the war when some of the ministers that were repatriated to Japan came back to Hawaii, that we were told that after the exchange was made, the Japanese ships landed at Saipan and the men, 18 years and older were dropped off there, given rifles with bayonets and were ordered to join the Japanese army to fight, even ministers and all of them with no military training. After we moved to Honolulu, one of the ministers, Rev. O., who had returned from Japan post-war, showed me bullet wound scars on his abdomen, which he got fighting in Saipan. For the mothers and children who went back to Japan on the repatriation ships and came back to Hawaii, stories of sadness of being separated again without their husbands, fathers, and this time for some, their sons and older brothers, of more worries and despair about the safety of their spouses or sons fighting at the front lines of war. (We also heard much later of a family whose son was killed in action in Saipan.) Then, after reaching Japan, they were thrown into a country deep in hardships of sufferings and shortages of food and jobs, which made us grateful that we had not been included twice to be sent back with them.)

It was August, 1945 when we could hear shoutings, loud music and fireworks from the neighboring town. The people in the town closest to our camp were celebrating America's victory and the sounds of the fireworks during the day became visible at night. We did not know what had happened until Bishop F. announced that evening that the war had ended and that Japan had lost! America had won this war! The men came back from hearing the news of the loss, stunned and walking slowly with heads bent in a dark, somber atmosphere, not talking to each other, smiling or laughing like they usually do. For many of them, it was hard to believe that Japan had surrendered and lost the war because the news was broadcasted by American newscasters on American radio, and Bishop F. could only repeat to them the announcement of what he had heard. Even I, a child, thought that Japan would win this war and release us from behind the barbed wires to freedom. Why not, when although being such a small nation, we learned in Japanese school history that Japan won wars against such large nations as China and Russia. We heard of the fearless Japanese soldiers who were willing to sacrifice their lives for their emperor and country, the (神風,) "Kamikaze," pilots that sacrificed their lives by deliberately becoming the human bombs by hitting their targets with their planes, and the soldiers whose parents when sending them off to war, tell them to die and come home, but not before achieving meritorious distinguished services for their country, to be proud of their heritage, not to shame the family name and their ancestors. There was a dark cloud of heaviness in the atmosphere and no laughter to be heard. There were many who could not believe that Japan had lost the war, or refused to believe that Japan could really, actually lose the war! Even I, as a child, did not dare to ask Father or Mother what was to become of us now, although I am certain all parents and some of the older children must have had the same thoughts also.

School began again after summer vacation and we were now 6th graders. With many of the teachers gone, sent back to Japan on the repatriation ships, our teacher again was the same kind, gentle, Mr. Fukuda from Hawaii, who was our 5th grade teacher. Yoshie's family had also not been listed to be repatriated and so we were still together. Clifford's family also was still at Crystal City and so I continued to play with his sister, K. I can't remember much of those months after the war ended as to what I did as the days went by, which of my friends I had played with, which of my friends had gone on the two ships, repatriated back to Japan.

As the days steeped into autumn, I missed the Maple tree leaves turning to orange and red for I don't remember even seeing too many trees except for the orange grove next to the triplex housing area and some trees here and there. It was cold during the winter months and so I know I did not go swimming. I was not asked to do household chores except to sometimes sweep out the rooms or to babysit the younger siblings. I know that I went to friends' homes to play for I was not one to sit at home unless I was given a chore to do or to study. I don't remember even telling my parents where I was going except that I was going to visit some friends. Going alone here and there within the camp was pretty much safe so they did not object to my going all over the camp. I always returned before mealtimes for I do not recall eating meals at a friend's home. I visited my older friends to chat with them, played with friends closer to my age on some weekends, afternoons after school or on holidays.

The days continued on without much differences and months had gone by. One day, our parents were called to the office, perhaps the camp administrator's office, although I did not know where it was located. They were asked whether they wanted to be sent to Japan or to return to where they had lived before being interned. This was being asked of everyone's parents and a decision had to be told to the administrator after thinking and discussing as to where the families wanted to go when being released from the internment camp. I heard my parents say that parents were notified that children 18 years old or older and were American citizens but chose to go back to Japan with them would not be allowed to return or enter the United States again.

My parents hardly had any arguments and if they did, it was not in the presence of us children because I was very surprised and anxious with their arguing about this issue. Father wanted to go back to Hawaii and find out if Japan had indeed lost the war and if so, we could send food back to Grandmother and sister Megumi. He argued that we could all return to Japan from Hawaii, that it was closer from there than from Texas, after learning the truth of the outcome of the war. He also felt that, if indeed Japan had lost the war, our family of 9 would be a burden on the war-torn country and its people. Instead, upon confirming the outcome of the war, Father stressed and insisted that we could send food back to Grandmother and Megumi. (As mentioned earlier, Megumi, our eldest sister, when she was 6 years old, had been sent to Japan from Maui for Grandmother Ko to raise.) Mother argued that she needed to know if Grandmother and Megumi were alive. We knew how stressed Mother felt or she would not have said to Father that Grandmother was HER mother, and Father replied that he was adopted by Mother's parents before he married her, so he did not have to comply according to her wishes of opting to return to Japan. Finally, Father told Mother that if she really wanted to go back to Japan to confirm that Grandmother and Megumi were alive, she could go back to Japan alone and that he would take the children and go back to Hawaii. Mother came back with the family since she did not want to part with us and Katsuyo was still an infant.

Some of the Hawaii ministers chose to return to Hawaii but some of them and many of the Mainland families chose to go back to Japan. I had not heard about what the Peru and other Latin American families had decided to do. When those of us returning to Hawaii left Crystal City Internment Camp in December, 1945, we were probably the first families to leave after the war ended.

Freedom from being behind tall barbed wired fences still did not mean anything yet for until we reached Honolulu, we still had to do whatever and go wherever we were ordered by the FBI agents to do. Riding the bus to the railroad station, getting on the train, passing near the El Paso town, our last ride on it took us to California, boarding the Navy ship, and then finally, we were on our way home to Hawaii. Other families, still many of them, remained in the camp. I guess they had to wait until arrangements could be made for them to go to their choices of destinations.

(The camp will remain open until the last families left, and was closed officially on February 27, 1948, nearly three more long years after the war ended in 1945. Years of confinement and loss of freedom, living according to the orders of the FBI and those in charge of the internees at Crystal City Internment Camp, may have ended when the doors and gates of the camp finally closed, with the guards with rifles in the towers gone, but the doors to the trauma and hardships impacted on all the families that were arrested and sent there will never close or be forgotten by all involved.)

(There was a big reunion at the California Casino in Las Vegas in 2001, the same year as the 9-11 disaster, only a week later. All of the Izumi sisters attended, with their daughters, for it was good for them to hear and see what we had gone through. It was great to meet old friends, buy memorabilia of the camp and to see photographs of events I read about, the yearly Las Vegas trips in May, arranged all those years by Toni Tomita (Tomoko Takeuchi,) that begin with the fun bus rides, the slot tournaments, dinners and the (新年宴会,) "Shinnen Enkais," New Year dinner parties enjoyed by the California group and wished that I could have been there with them. Thanks to Sumi's Crystal City Chatter, I have been kept in touch with the Crystal City groups' goings- on, the latest news and old news, good advices on health and helpful subjects, fun sayings and jokes. I also read the articles and stories written by her and others about their experiences in the internment and relocation camps and saw the differences of their hardships and sufferings as compared to mine because of the differences in our ages. For the boys and girls in their teens, they had every right to be resentful of the harsh treatments, loss of freedom, their homes and rights as American citizens and felt the anguish much more deeply than a child of 8 years old that I was. It is a wonder and gratifying how Sumi has held us together all these years with her diligent, interesting and entertaining writings in the Crystal City Chatter, and Toni has headed committees for the annual Las Vegas trips and other events. (有難う,すみさん!!,) "Arigato, Sumi-san!!," Thank you, Sumi-san!! (有難う、トーニさん!!,) "Arigato, Toni―san!!" Thank you, Toni-san!!)

(There will be the very last Crystal City Internment Camp reunion in Las Vegas this coming October 20-21, 2015, thanks to Toni again chairing the committee making all the arrangements. It is gratifying that there is to be a reunion and understandable that it will our last reunion, for children born at the camp during our confinement are now in their 70s and for us, fortunately to be healthy enough to attend, are octogenarians and nonagenarians. My sister, Norie Freitas, was 7 years old when we left Crystal City. We asked our sister-in-law, Robyn Izumi, to join us and we are looking forward to meeting the Crystal City friends there.)

(Attending the reunion was very nostalgic and it was wonderful to meet with friends made in the internment camp. I could not wait to see them again and so Norie and I stood on the sidewalk where the buses would arrive. Toni Tomita, being the chairperson of the committee for this reunion, was the first to get off the bus. She recognized me right away and we hugged each other joyfully. She efficiently organized the front desk registration by getting the keys and room numbers to the waiting attendees who then got off the bus, picked up their luggage and went directly to their rooms. This must have been the way she did things at the annual Las Vegas reunions in May but I was very impressed how she so effortlessly went about handling so many people, all at once. Of course, this did not surprise me for I always knew how "shan shan" (go-getter) at how she did things, for she gave me this impression in camp, as a child, even then, just with her aura.).

Toni Tomita giving instruction on "Internees Bingo"

(It was also wonderful to meet Sumi Shimatsu and she immediately gave me the same impression as Toni did, intelligent, witty and efficient. No wonder she wrote the Crystal City Chatter for so many years. Her daughter, Paula, just like her, friendly and helpful, along with Toni, was efficiently making sure that things went smoothly at this reunion. Sumi also arranged to have Ms. Jan Jarboe Russell, author of "Train to Crystal City," be the keynote speaker at our reunion. Sumi's family's experience of relocation and internment is written in Ms. Russell's book on the section of the West Coast Japanese hardships and being sent to various camps before settling at Crystal City Internment Camp.)

Sumi Shimatsu introducing Ms. Russell

61

(Meeting Ms. Jan Jarboe Russell, author of "Train to Crystal City" and guest speaker at the reunion, having her sign my book with a personal note was gratifying and she left me encouraging words, "Keep on writing," which also made me feel good about writing the "Izumi Story," our family's stay and my perspective as a child confined behind barbed wires with guards in high towers with rifles.

To really be a part and experience the camaraderie of the internees, she flew from Texas to Los Angeles and rode the bus with the attendees from there. She could be seen intermingling cheerfully and friendly with everyone and even joined in the "Bon odori" dance to the song, (炭鉱節) "Tankou Bushi, ") a folksong about a mining town in Japan. She made us feel as though we knew her because of her book and her empathy for us.)

(Her book is very informative and full of related details of governmental movements and documentations of proclamations and orders that initiated the mass arrests from the West Coast and Latin American countries, of Japanese, German and Italian aliens that were considered enemies and a danger to the security of our country, America. Hardships, not only of the Japanese aliens and their American citizen children that were arrested but of the German internees' hardships are written so vividly and will forever be recorded as part of the disgrace and inhuman happenings that befell those that were confined in relocation centers and in our internment camp. Stories in excerpts that even I, as an internee of Crystal City Internment Camp, did not know about because of being a child, am now gratified to know more about the camp by reading her book as an adult. People that were in charge and operated the camp, the English school teachers that came from outside, their names and duties, the way the Germans lived in their side of the camp, etc., because of Ms. Russell's book, "Train to Crystal City," many things were brought to light for me and, I am sure, for many others who were children during those years of confinement there in Texas.)

Keynote speaker, Ms. Jan Jarboe Russell

(I was saddened to hear from Tayeko Ogawa Kurashige's niece that she was unable to come to the reunion because she had not fully recovered from her recent ailment. I had looked forward to meeting her again. Although I was disappointed because Taye could not be with us at this reunion, I was relieved to hear that she was feeling better. I got to meet her sister, Kazuko Tajii, and niece. I gave my address to her niece and asked her to give my best regards to Taye and to tell her that I would be writing her soon.)

(Blanca Maoki Katsura and another of Father's student told me that they remembered Father very well. They said that he was a strict teacher but was the "best story-teller" and had beautiful calligraphy, although written on the blackboard. It was unexpected and gratifying to hear them mention Father and made me feel happy and proud to be his daughter for they addressed me as "Izumi Sensei's" daughter when they saw my name tag. I was happy when Blanca said she remembered me from camp but I only remembered her and her sister Libia Maoki Yamamoto's last name, Maoki, which was familiar when I saw the list of attendees sent out by Toni before the reunion. Libia asked after my sister, Junko, who she said was her classmate at Japanese school in camp. The sisters, originally from Peru, were very friendly and it was a pleasure to meet them.)

(I was happy to meet Chieko Kamisato again for I remembered her very well from when we were in the camp. We gave each other our e-mail addresses and promised to keep in touch. She looked the same and I was able to recognize her. Friendships formed when sharing the same situations can also be binding, as I found out upon meeting friends after 70 years and also those I had met during the 2001 reunion. I was very impressed to learn that Chieko, after moving to Los Angeles, studied English, attended school to become a successful fashion designer and owner of a clothing factory to manufacture her designs. I can imagine the continued hardships she must have endured to achieve her goals.)

(I had looked forward to meeting Ruby and Betty Fukunaga again after 14 years for we had met at the 2001 reunion. Betty immediately remembered me as we hugged each other but I was very sad to hear that Ruby had passed on. I will always remember her warm friendship in camp, slim and tall with her long braided hair. We shared many "girl talks" when I visited their home and she was also a close friend.)

(Maru Okazaki Hiratzka looked the same as when we met in 2001 and I was happy to see her again. We talked about Toki and me going to her home, also in the D-duplex section and reminisced about camp days. She remembered the Fukuda sisters from Hawaii and I was happy to tell her that they are well.)

(Thanks to Toni and her committee, it was a wonderful and successful reunion. 50 internees and some of their spouses, children, grandchildren. 3rd generation "Sanseis" had come to this reunion.)

(Some of the "Sanseis" had served on the committee to help Toni make this reunion a great one. For us in our 80s and 90s, to have them take part in our history of internment, means that what we went through will not be forgotten for they will have learned about them and will tell it to their children and others.)

(Although we all knew it would be the last one where we would all gather, nonetheless, it was not sad but helped to put a closure to the hardships endured by all of us, and to finally put our hearts and minds to be at ease in our memories as those internment days were taped during the "Circle of Friends," to be forever recorded, never to be forgotten. The one and most gratifying thing about what happened to all of us because of the war and confined at Crystal City Internment Camp was the friendships born there, which have endured and lasted more than 70 years and to remain forever throughout our lives. Happy to renew our friendships, many of us exchanged addresses and e-mail addresses and promised to keep in touch with each other.)

CHAPTER 6

END OF THE WAR! RETURNING TO HAWAII

For those of us returning to Hawaii, we again rode on a train to California. If I recalled correctly, as we boarded the U.S. Navy ship, I saw the name, USS Comet on its broadside. We were being transported back to Honolulu from the naval base in San Diego. Far differently from the ship we sailed on when we were sent to San Francisco in 1942, we were very uncomfortable on this navy ship, with the mothers, babies and daughters sleeping on hung hammock-like beds, the fathers and sons were sleeping on mats in the very bottom part of the ship. We could meet on deck but as usual, I was seasick most of the trip and was miserable. The smell of the diesel oil was strong and made me feel queasy and nauseous. The Comet was a smaller built ship and rocked roughly in high seas.

As we disembarked and stepped onto the soil of Honolulu, at last, the first taste of true freedom dawned on us. No more FBI agents that were gone from the time we boarded the USS Comet with no means of escaping from the ship on an ocean, perhaps the crew watched us, no one to tell us what to do or where to go. The clean sweet air with the tropical breezes, the hibiscus and plumeria blossoms, the swaying coconut trees, all familiar sights were nostalgic, and seemed to welcome us home. Although it was December when we left Texas and it would still be very cold in Crystal City, here in Hawaii, we did not even need to wear sweaters and the weather was very nice, with tropical breezes and clear blue skies, just as we remembered. This return to Hawaii may have ended our years of hardships, anxieties, separations from loved ones, confinement and loss of freedom in the camp, but awaiting us were the aftereffects of the war, the hardships and sufferings impacts that were to befall upon us, and definitely also upon the Mainland families that had been arrested and taken to the internment camp and other relocation camps, and most definitely more so, what awaited the families that chose to return to Japan, a war-torn country from the bombings, with shortages of food, jobs and necessities.

Upon arrival at Honolulu, we were met by Mr. Fujii of the Fujii Store and Mr. Takeuchi of the Takeuchi Hotel, who used to live in Papaaloa. They had been staunch and supportive leaders among the members of our congregation before the war at the Papaaloa Hongwanji Mission, as well as helpful advisors to Father when he was newly assigned to the temple there. We were very happy and surprised to see them for we did not know about their moving to Honolulu but, just as they had at Papaaloa, they were willingly here to continue their support of our family. Father and his work done at the Papaaloa Hongwanji Mission for the five months three weeks prior to his being arrested and how Mother and Takaaki took over the work of the temple for the congregation before leaving to join Father, could have impressed favorably upon these two wonderful men who had come again to aid us.

We went to the Kobayashi Hotel, which was then located on Beretania Street near the Aala Park and Father registered for rooms there. (As I write this, it just occurred to me that Mr. Fujii and Mr. Takeuchi must have paid for the rooms, and I would not be surprised if they gave him some money to buy food when we got to Father's next designated assignment. After all, Father had not earned even a cent of income for four long years while being confined.)

We then went to the Hawaii Betsuin (Main temple and headquarters in Hawaii) of the Honpa Hongwanji Mission on Fort Street (now Pali Hwy.) Father was told by the Bishop that we would return to the Papaaloa Hongwanji Mission on the Big Island, where he had been previously assigned when the war began.

With a family of 9 members, Mr. Takeuchi took Hiromichi to stay the night at his home and Mr. Fujii took me, Tomoko, to his home.

Mr. Fujii was a tall, big, kind man and he told me that I should take a nice, warm bath and relax after 5 days of being on a ship. I went into the (風呂場,) "furoba," bathhouse, which was a separate building with a short, covered walkway to and from the house. There was a big wooden "furo," Japanese bathtub filled with clean hot water. I was so happy that I soaped myself and without even hesitating, jumped into the "furo." To my dismay, the water turned white and soapy and too late, I remembered that I should have rinsed the soap off myself before soaking in the clean water of the "furo". The long years since leaving Hawaii in 1942, and having taking only showers thereafter, made me forget how one should take a bath in a "furo." I was afraid to tell Mr. Fujii what I had done but being the kind and caring person that he was, he only laughed and said it was not such a big deal. He understood after being told that I had forgotten how to take a bath in a "furo", and in my delight to be able to soak and sit in a tub, made me hurry to enjoy being up to my neck in the nice, just right, hot water.

When Mr. Fujii drove me to the Kobayashi Hotel the next morning, Hiromichi was already there with Mr. Takeuchi. They kindly drove us to the pier where we were to board an Inter-island boat to Hilo, on the Big Island of Hawaii.

CHAPTER 7

PAPAALOA HONGWANJI MISSION, ISLAND OF HAWAII

We boarded an Inter-island boat and sailed overnight to Hilo harbor. I can't remember who came to meet us and drove us back to Papaaloa, but there must have been at least two cars for the 9 of us and our luggage. It was very nostalgic to come back to our home again and as we walked in the large front yard where (盆,) "Bon," dances, yearly dances at (盆会,) "Bon-e," a Buddhist memorial festival to remember those who passed on were held, I noticed beautiful purple flowers flowing down several stems from the palm tree, just before the steps to the house. I was amazed to see this for I had never seen such sweet, fragrant flowers before. Later I found out that someone had planted Honohono orchids in the indentations on the palm tree bark and that they were not flowers of the palm. (To this day, Honohono orchid with its lovey scent and lavender purple petals is my favorite flower.) As you can see in the photo, the Azalea plant that was a shorter bush had grown taller than Mother while we were away.

Since the minister's residence was not ready for us to move in, we stayed with the Aoki family for a week or so while Father and the members of the congregation were getting our house ready for occupancy. Just as the last four years of confinement had deprived Father of an income, for the temple that had been deprived of their minister, the treasury was also at a standstill from the time we left to be interned. We stayed at the Aoki's home until Father could buy a stove and refrigerator. He must have borrowed the money for although there was furniture in the house, perhaps from the long years of no one living there, the stove and refrigerator were gone. As soon as they were bought, we moved in to settle in the house, and finally felt that we had truly come home.

There was a shortage of Hongwanji ministers after the war because some had been repatriated during the war, some chose to go back to Japan after the war, as did some of the ministers from other Relocation Centers. Father was assigned to Honohina Hongwanji, which had villages from Umauma, Honohina Mauka, Honohina, Ninole, and Kaikea. There was a branch temple in Ninole and so he had to perform services both at the temple in Honohina and Ninole on Sundays after the service at the Papaaloa Hongwanji. Laupahoehoe villages were Maulua, Kapehu, Papaaloa, Kihalani, Laupahoehoe, Kiilau, Puulai, Waipunalei and Ookala

The Azalea plant had grown taller than Mother while we were away.   *Rev. Kakusho Izumi, 1945*

Father began by collecting membership fees from the congregation members, to organize the Sunday school, Y.B.A, (Young Buddhist Association,) adult services and memorial services. The offertories for the services he conducted were supplemental to his salary. The membership fee was not mandatory and there was no set amount listed per month and so whatever the member could afford was accepted. In the countryside of the outer islands in those days, people could afford only minimal amounts. Thus, began our financial hardships from day one of our return, mainly due to the lack of income for the past 4 years.

(Even after returning to Hawaii, we did not anticipate the consequences and hardships from being interned and confined in the camp all those years would continue on for years, even after the older children graduated from high school with some of us giving up going to college or universities because of the financial difficulties that were still ongoing.)

Coming back to an empty home, first of all, Father had to buy the necessary things like the stove and the refrigerator. We could not afford an electric stove so he bought a kerosene stove with three burners. We hung a bottle of kerosene on the side of the stove, and had to lift and lean the chimney-like covers with glass windows that were over the wicks, and lean them onto the holes directly behind them to start the fire by lighting it with a match to the kerosene-soaked wicks. Turning the knob up or down to regulate the fire strength and covering the wick again, we can then start the cooking. The kerosene was delivered by C.M. whenever we called him for a refill of the 50-gallon barrel outside of the bathhouse, near the downstairs kitchen of the temple, where the (婦人会,) "Fujinkai," Women's Club members gathered to cook for temple events, weddings, and funerals.

Having to go to Honohina which was far from Pappaloa, another thing Father said he immediately needed was a car. Again, after being interned in the camp all those years, he had no money to buy one. He came home after a few days with an old black, rectangular box-shaped car with steps. The horn was a small round button in the middle of the steering wheel and when pressed, tooted a sound like "ahgooga," which made me laugh whenever I heard it. His friend from Honomu gave the car to him. Just by looking at it, you could see the vintage of that old car but it really served its purpose, and even took us to Hilo when Father often made trips to the library there for us. We had a small library in Papaaloa but we had read most of the books there and so, loving education, he did not mind driving all that way to Hilo when we needed to borrow books and return them. (After months of working, Father bought a Studebaker. The car was a large, comfortable sedan and we rode it until we left Papaaloa. It was a good car but the Packard-Studebaker company stopped making cars many years ago and no longer exists.)

Our Studebaker

On the right side of the temple was a narrow lane that led to the back of the temple where the homes of the Taketas, Kubos, and 3 Chinese men that had retired from the plantation stood. Beyond that lane and alongside of the temple, and behind the Shikuma home, the plantation had built a huge garage after we left in 1942. Maintenance and repair work on the trucks and equipment were done in the long, corrugated-roofed building, and in front of it was the big, wide cleared ground area, where the trucks and equipment were parked when work was over each day.

A truck driver and member of our temple, Seiko K., was always kind to us when we did see him after work on his way home, he used to playfully tease us children. One day, Hiromichi teased him back by calling him "Senko, Penko." Seiko, laughing, started chasing him for fun, when Hiromichi fell down on the sidewalk of the bridge between our home and the Plantation Store, and fractured his arm. (Among our siblings, he was the only one who suffered arm and leg fractures, which would be the reason why, years later after moving to Honolulu, our parents did not give consent for him to be a football player when he was in high school.) Seiko felt very sorry and bad about the fracture, but I assured him that it was not his fault and that I would explain to our parents how it happened. Hiromichi had to have his arm casted at the plantation hospital by Dr. F.

On the first 1946, New Year's Day in Papaaloa, as was the Japanese custom, after getting up and washing our faces, brushing our teeth, the first thing we did, as we always had done every year, was to wish our parents, (明けまして、新年おめでとうございます。今年も宜しくお願い致します。) "Akemashite Shinnen Omedeto gozaimasu. Kotoshi mo yoroshiku onegai itashimasu," Congratulations for a Happy New Year and please continue to care for us in this New Year, bowing in respect.

We visited homes of the members of the congregation to say our New Year's greetings, to enjoy the wonderful food prepared in each home, which was the custom in a Japanese home, to welcome guests to celebrate the New Year in and partake the (お節料理、) "Osechi ryouri," New Year dishes together.

I always enjoyed going to the Ikemoto home since their daughter, Momoe, was my very first friend when we moved to Papaaloa from Kilauea, Kauai in June, 1941. She was called Momo and although my name is Tomoko, everyone called me Tomo. I thought it was cool that our names rhymed, Momo and Tomo. Momo and I played together a lot and her mother would send me home after giving us a "furo" bath. The water would be white with the sulfur-containing liquid she poured in, telling us that this was good for the skin.

They had a (鯉、) "Koi," carp pond right outside of the kitchen door, stone steps leading up to the back yard where there was an area fenced in with meshed wire and a chicken coop where chicken and roosters were raised. Her older sisters used to help my Mother by babysitting us before the war. Now, again, they and Sawae S. also helped with babysitting the younger siblings as Mother had to teach Japanese school, flower arrangement, and tea ceremony, as well as organize the "Fujinkai" Women's Club of the temple.

On January 2nd, after having lunch at the Ikemotos, I told Momo that I swam in a pool at the internment camp but that I had never forgotten the fun we had swimming in the gulch behind the Egusa's home called Egusa Pond. We decided to go swimming and we went to change into my swimsuit and get a towel from home. As she and I started to walk across the street towards the gulch, Norie, 7, being 5 years younger than me, wanted to come along, and to run away from her, we ran as fast as we could. Right before we reached one of the homes leading to the path of the gulch, I tripped and fell on a rock. Without realizing that I had a big gash on my left knee, I quickly got up and started to run again when I felt a flapping on my leg with a warm wetness. Looking down at my knee, I saw white cartilage hanging down from the deep laceration, with a lot of bleeding. I called out to Momo, who was running ahead, and she came back to where I was standing. Having seen my injury, she grabbed hold of my arm and rushed me back home. Scooping up the cartilage and holding it against my knee with my left hand, with Momo's help in keeping my balance, I hobbled my way back home. Perhaps, my knee was numb due to the impact of the fall, I did not feel a thing until we reached part of the sidewalk leading to the temple, when out of nowhere, it seemed as though pain shot throughout my entire body, and I just sat down and shouted for Father. He came running out and seeing my open wound, carried me and sat me down on the steps of the old car that had being parked in the yard. Bringing out gauzes, bandages and plaster, he poured a whole bottle of Hydrogen Peroxide on the wound, bandaged it, and drove me to the Laupahoehoe Plantation Hospital.

Dr. F. was away and was to return from the Paauilo Clinic. The nurse cleaned and disinfected the wound, which was very painful, bandaged it, and told me that we had to wait for the doctor. When he returned, he said he was going to suture the wound and asked the nurse if she had given me any numbing shots. He glared at her when she said she did not. After giving me the pain shots to numb the area, he sutured seven stitches there, splinted the knee to immobilize it from bending, and gave me a Tetanus Toxoid immunization shot.

Instead of returning to Kapehu Elementary School as a 12-year old, because students at that age were supposed to enter the seventh grade as an Intermediate school student, I started my first day at the Laupahoehoe High and Elementary School, with my leg in a splint. Mother had decided that the younger siblings would ride the bus to school with Junko. Because of my injury, until the stitches and the splint were removed, I got to ride the bus.

I had attended Japanese school during those internment years at Crystal City, but the principal, Mr. F., decided to start me in the fourth grade, because I was in the third grade when we left to join our Father in 1942. I told him that I had already learned my multiplication, division, and decimals, although in the metric system, he said that because I was in the third grade when we left Hawaii, I now belonged in the fourth grade. Without even giving any of our siblings or me placement tests, my brothers and sisters were also put into lower grades rather than the grades they should have been in.

Miss D.D. was a pretty, young teacher from Ohio. That year, there were teachers from the Mainland, most of them in their early twenties, and all of them such beauties, that they could be movie stars. I loved to peek into their classrooms and see them when I walked along the corridors fronting each room, and gave them a big smile whenever we passed each other on the corridor in front of the classrooms. Their beauty made me feel very nice and happy. It was a joy to see them, they were that beautiful!

That first morning, before classes began and roll had been called, I was asked by Ms. D. to lead the class in the Pledge of Allegiance, but found that I had forgotten some of the words to it. I explained to Miss D. about the three years four months of being confined in

North Carolina, and in an internment camp in Crystal City, Texas during the war, because fathers who had immigrated to America from Japan, Germany and Italy, were thought to be dangerous aliens to the security of our country, and were arrested to be repatriated to their respective countries in exchange for Americans interned there. (Although I attended Japanese school, I do not think that the English School teachers in Crystal City Internment Camp, under the circumstances, made the students recite the Pledge of Allegiance to the flag of the United States.)

Ms. D. seemed surprised and did not know anything about what had happened to us internees. (This incident about the internment must have impressed her for she wrote about it in a letter to her parents. Later, when her father published a book from letters received from Ms. D., my forgetting the Pledge of Allegiance was written in it. Recently, I had the opportunity to meet Mrs. Marsue McShane, the former Ms. McGinnis who at the time lived in the same cottage as Ms. D. She said that the beautiful teachers that year had just graduated from college and came to Hawaii to teach but that they had no idea of those internment camps or relocation camps and she learned about them when after the war, the people in Laupahoehoe were so happy that the minister, Izumi, had come back from the camp to their temple. She did not know that I was an Izumi and when I told her that I was Father's daughter, I mentioned also that I was very surprised that she had remembered Father's name after 70 years had elapsed. She replied that because she had heard it mentioned happily everywhere many times by the people, she always remembered the reverend that had returned to the Papaaloa temple from the internment camp was Minister Izumi. Ms. McShane looked incredibly well and young for she was now in her 90's and although she walked with a cane, her mind was sharp and told us stories of her stay in Laupahoehoe and an update of some happenings after leaving there.)

The lessons in the fourth grade were so easy, and it felt rather strange to be among other students much younger. My classmates were the same age as Hiromichi, three years younger than myself. I felt silly to have to lie on a mat, and take a nap after lunch, before our afternoon classes. I always chose the spot near the door. I did not fall asleep but just lay there and rested.

One day, looking out the door during nap time, I was surprised to see a black dog saunter by and a bare-footed boy just behind it. (In September, when I was placed in the 7th grade, I met Wilfred, a classmate and son of one of the teachers, Mr. Laeha, and learned that he and his pet dog were a familiar sight in school.)

Although I was never a student in his class, one of the pleasures I remember while attending Laupahoehoe School was that Mr. Laeha knew that I loved music, and he used to invite me to sit on the doorsteps of his home, to listen to him sing Hawaiian songs. He would ask me what instrument I would like for him to play and I could choose from the ukulele, guitar or mandolin. He had a beautiful voice and his enjoyment in singing made those times memorable. To this day, songs like Anapaula, Naka Puueo, Nalani, Kaulana Hilo Hanakahi, Hawaiian War Chant, Yellow Ginger Lei, Lovely Hula Hands and many other songs replay in my mind, still remembered. Many Laupahoehoe students that sing Hawaiian songs learned them from Mr. Laeha. His daughter, Kawaihona, treated me as a sister and they are my (hanai,) "adopted" Hawaiian family.

(We have not met for quite some years, but Kawaihona and her husband, Tommy Poy, still keep in touch and I will always visit them when I go to the Big Island. My husband, Raf, and Tommy became fast friends from when they first met.)

A terrible tragedy occurred on April 1, 1946. The tsunami that hit the Hawaiian Islands in nearly 100 years ended in a traumatic disaster causing major damages and casualties on all of the islands. A big earthquake in the Aleutian Islands brought the tidal wave to Hawaii. Laupahoehoe High and Elementary School was located in an area that was at sea level, with the teachers' cottages all in a row, closer to the seashore. The athletic field with the bleachers was closer to the beginning of the grounds on the right side, and in front of the shop where woodwork was taught, with the boys' and girls' toilets further up closer to the school, on the left side of the grounds. Beyond the elementary classrooms was the field that grew the plants the Agriculture class had planted. Higher above the garden was the principal's cottage.

(I was not at the scene of the tidal wave as it was called in those days. My version of the tidal wave as it happened is from the various stories told to me by several people and so if all is not fact, please also remember that I am writing this by recalling what happened when I was 12 years old.)

The teachers were in their pajamas and having breakfast, when the first wave came into the cottages, which made them come out to the grounds to see what was happening. The buses that brought the students to the school started by picking up the students from the farthest communities, Honohina and Ookala and so some of those students, as well as some others that were already there, climbed onto the bleachers, seeing the waves washing onto the school grounds. The second wave brought fishes that were flip-flopping around the grounds which made some of the students run down to see this most unusual sight. Meanwhile, the teachers went back into the cottages to change and to get ready for school when the third and biggest wave hit. Gone were the cottages, not a single item or plumbing left, just a flat slab of concrete to show that houses once stood there. The huge wave gobbled up the boy's toilet, part of the shop building, and the bleachers with the students on it, sweeping them all along the way, together with the children still fascinated by the fishes on the field, as the devastating wave gushed back into the now empty sandy floor bottom left by the receding sea that had built up into a huge, big, high mountain of tidal wave, and dashed against the jutting lava rocks, back into the ocean in ebb tide. No one knew what a tidal wave was. April 1st, being April Fools' Day, perhaps did not help to warn of the danger and disaster either. 24 lives were lost, 16 students, 3 of the beautiful teachers, 1 male teacher, and 4 members of a teacher's family.

Many students from Papaaloa walked the long miles to school. From Puulai on, the road was all downhill until we reached the straight road leading to the school, with houses on both sides, including the Laeha home, and the grounds at the same level as the sea.

I usually walked down with Ronald Yamaoka, his sister, Fumi and some other students. Ronald was washed out into the sea by the tidal wave, but was rescued by Dr. F. later that afternoon, who went out on a boat to look for survivors with F. Malani, who knew the tide and waves of that ocean and navigated the boat as to when and how and which direction it should sail. The owner of the boat was from the Waimea area and the other man that helped to cut the end of the boat, and attached an engine to it for faster movement and on its own power, rather than to depend on the wind and waves, was the fourth person. They rescued and brought back Ronald, Yoshio A., and Ms. Marsue McGinnis, the girls' physical education teacher, whom Dr. F. later married.

Herbert Nishimoto, Takashi T., and Asao K., were rescued the following day after climbing onto a raft dropped off by a search plane, and floated all the way to the Kohala coast. (I found out just this January by reading the interview Herbert had given the University of Hawaii reporter, that after being swept out to sea, rather than trying to get back to shore, which is what most people may do, he swam farther toward the deeper sea instead of trying to swim back to shore and getting hurt by being dashed against the many lava rocks jutting along the area nearer to the shore. Being a boy scout, he had exercised and strengthened himself by swimming and was a strong swimmer.

He was floating on the makeshift raft he had made by gathering some debris with a board that had nails in it. For a hammer, he had used the axe handle he had found floating nearby. As he floated where the waves were taking him, along the way, he saw Takashi and Asao floating, hanging on to the floating debris. He brought them onto his raft. He did not remember which of the boys he handed the long lumber to and pulled him in and which one he swam out and brought to his raft. He made sure the boys would not be washed off by the waves as they slept on the raft in utter weariness. Herbert swam to secure the rubber raft dropped off later by a rescue plane, inflated it, and helped the two boys move into it. Only after helping them onto the rubber raft did Herbert also get some rest.

I found his home telephone number listed and called him at his home after reading his version of a survivor, because I remembered him, but, being older, he did not remember me. When I told him I was the minister's daughter, he remembered my Father. I gathered some classmates, including Ronald and Ms. McShane nee Ms. McGinnis, and we met Herbert for lunch on Friday, January 30, 2015. With three survivors of the tidal wave there, stories of their experiences and recues were retold as we also were recalling happenings of that tragic day.) Mrs. A., whose home was near the shore, and _. Murakami were rescued by a military ship and landed at Hilo Harbor. They were all the fortunate survivors that had been swept out to sea but were miraculously saved.

Ms. Marsue McShane, neé Ms. McGinnis

It must have been fate, our Karma, for I had the starting of a cold, no fever, just runny nose and a slight cough. I rode the bus that day. The bakery lady, Mrs. T., who delivered bread every school day, stopped our bus, warned the driver about the disaster. The 2-way lane road was narrow with the mountain on the left and the high cliff on the right, whose drop ended in the ocean with dashing waves breaking at the bottom. A short thick metal fence ran along the side of the cliff. The driver had to go back and forth many times to turn the bus around and send us home again. Had we walked to school on that day, I would have been together with Ronald, and may have been washed out with him by the tidal wave.

I volunteered at the hospital for some of the survivors were hospitalized from injuries sustained from the tidal wave. Dark, somber, sad days followed that tragic day but many were thankful that they had survived.

As the days went by, bodies were washed up to shore, Father went with the families to identify them, and funeral services were held. Father could hardly chant the sutras for his voice broke nearly to a sob, as he sadly mourned with the families and the entire communities for the young victims.

Some of the victims' bodies were never recovered. The entire communities were in mourning. One day, a member of our congregation came to see Father, and told him that his only child's body was lost, and he had no grave to pray or to put flowers there for his son at "O-bon." He did not want to pray to the ocean that took his son. Father resolved at that moment to build a monument for the victims.

Father went knocking on doors, house to house from Honohina to Ookala, asking for donations in order to erect the monument. He then ordered a marble memorial tablet with all the names and ages of the victims carved on it by his friend, a stonecutter in Hilo, who made grave stones. He asked the then County Chairman, Mr. J. K., for permission to use the land down at the Laupahoehoe Point, to lay the monument there. The Chairman, who came to many Young Buddhist Association conferences to extend congratulatory speeches, was Father's friend. He offered to build a platform with steps and a dais so that the monument could be placed higher up from the ground, and with enough walking space for people to place flowers, and to stand before it in prayer. It was dedicated at the joint memorial service held by our Buddhist temple and both the Christian and Catholic churches in the community on April 1st, 1947.

(After his retirement, Father was invited to attend the 80th anniversary of the founding of the Papaaloa Hongwanji. He, Mother and I flew from Honolulu to this celebratory service, and Mr. and Mrs. H. Shima kindly invited us to stay overnight at their home. The following morning, Father took a walk with me and stopped at all the Hongwanji members' homes in the neighborhood and chanted a sutra and prayed at their altars, remembering their parents, now gone, but had been members of his congregation. The children that were Young Buddhist Association members were now the parents but were happy to see Father again. After those home services, before returning to Honolulu, Father asked me to take him to pray at the monument. At that time, he said that this monument would be the perpetual evidence of his ministerial work there in the Laupahoehoe district, when all else is gone.)

Rev. Kakusho Izumi at the 1946 tsunami monument

(When Miwako Miura Tsuruda, my best friend, and I were visiting the monument on one of our class reunions held at Laupahoehoe, a tourist standing before the monument, asked us if we knew any of the people whose names are on the monument. When I told her that the monument was erected by Father with donations from parents in the communities, it was this tourist who told me that this information should have been put there on a plaque below the monument because it is all part of the history of what happened on that tragic tsunami day, and the victims will be remembered forever because of the monument. At her words, I wished that the thought about putting a tiny plaque on the dais, saying that the monument was erected by the efforts of Rev. Kakusho Izumi and the communities had been already placed. However, when I tried to have this done, with the help of "hanai sister", Kawaihona Laeha Poy and her contacting the tsunami committee head, all efforts came to nil because the then members of the Papaaloa Hongwanji were not able to confirm this. Their reply was that the County had built the monument since they remembered seeing them build the platform for it. In a sense, who can blame them for thinking that, for they did not know that their parents, who have then long since passed away, were the donors, together with Father, helped to erect the tidal wave victims' monument. My thoughts, when I was given the reason why my wish was denied, was that there were many victims on the island of Hawaii from that tsunami, and the taxpayers would not agree for the County to build a monument only for those that died at Laupahoehoe School. As the minister of some of the families that lost their children, Father, after hearing Mr. S.'s sad words, had the monument built in memory of all those that died so tragically in the tsunami. Because Father was a kind, caring, humble person, never boastful, always putting his congregation and work even before his family, I consoled myself that he would not mind my failure to put his name there. By writing of how the monument was built here through his efforts, I feel the satisfaction that his deed will be remembered through his and my books.)

(Father was a poet and he always had paper and a pen in his shirt pocket, and whenever he saw something that inspired him, it was a familiar sight many times, to see him jotting down a poem that came into his thoughts. ("新万葉集,) "Shin Manyou shu," a new book of poetry in the form of "Tanka", words written in stanzas, 5,7,5,7,7 was published in Japan and Father's two poems are included in this 1938, issue. He was 35 years old at the time, and was assigned to the Kilauea Hongwanji when he submitted his two "Tanka" poems that appear in this prestigious book.

(布哇の生活、) "H a w a i i no Seikatsu," Life in Hawaii

(坦々たる舗装道路の両側に咲き続きたりハイビスカスの花)
  "Tantan taru hosou douro no ryougawa ni
saki tsuzuki tari haibisukasu no hana"
  On both sides of the fenced paved road, are continuous
  rows of hibiscus blossoms

(お布施を得て開封する時金高に心かかわる我は僧なり)
  "Ofuse wo ete kaifuu suru toki kindaka ni
kokoro kakawaru ware wa sou nari"
  Opening the envelope, my heart is concerned at
        the amount of the offeratory money enclosed, I am a priest)

(His New Year's Emperor's chosen-theme poem, which is an annual event, won second prize one year until months later, the first prize winner's poem was found to have been plagiarized, and so he was elated to be notified that he was the first prize winner. Although the notification came months after the award ceremony had taken place at the Imperial Palace in Japan, Father was satisfied and happy that he had won.)

(Years later, after moving to Honolulu, Father did publish 3 books on Buddhist teachings, newspaper articles and some personal experiences that applied to the teachings titled, (仏桑華,) "Bussoge,") Buddhist flower, Hibiscus in 1953, (続仏桑華,) "Zoku Bussoge,) Sequel to Bussoge, also at the same time in 1953 and (芬陀利華,) "Fundarike," written in Japanese characters for "Pundarika" meaning White Lotus in Sanskrit, in 1958. Father and I went to the Chinese temple in China town to meet a visiting high priest from one of the temples in Hong Kong. He gave Father a scroll with a Buddhist teaching written with a bamboo brush. The last Chinese characters in that teaching ended with "Pundarika." Father used those 4 characters to name his third book, "Fundarike," as pronounced in Japanese. These 3 books were put together from the manuscripts of sermons he broadcasted once a week for 20 years, from several different Japanese radio stations, for members of the congregations on Oahu and all of the outer islands that could not attend the Sunday services at the various Hongwanji temples.)

(Father was first introduced by a member of the temple, to KGU, the radio station. Two hours were set aside for Japanese broadcasts every day. Father was asked to give a religious lecture for approximately 5-6 minutes from around 10:15 a.m. every Tuesday morning. These sermons were gratefully and generously sponsored personally by Mr. S. H., the owner of the Hosoi Mortuary. Father's sermons on the radio were heard on all of the islands. Over the 20 years of Buddhist lectures he aired, he broadcasted them also from KGMB, KOHO and KZOO.)

(One day, a Mrs. N. visiting her son in Honolulu from Maui, came to our home on Lusitana Street to meet Father and thanked him for those broadcasts. My classmate, Tsuyako, also told me how much her mother, Mrs. Tanaka, loved my Father's sermons and looked forward to listening to them every week. Mr. Tanaka was one of the staunch supporters of Father at the Papaaloa Hongwanji Mission, as were some of the other members of the congregation that originally came from hometowns in Hiroshima, which was also where Father's hometown was. Tsuyako's sister, Elsie, was a classmate of my sister, Norie, and we were all so happy to see each other again after 62 years when Elsie visited Hawaii from Florida where she now lives. After returning to Florida, Elsie sent me the book, "Train to Crystal City" written by author, Jan Jarboe Russell, as a gift, because Father's broadcasted sermons made her mother happy as she looked forward to it every Tuesday morning for years, saying that she enjoyed hearing Father's sermons even though he was no longer living in Papaaloa.)

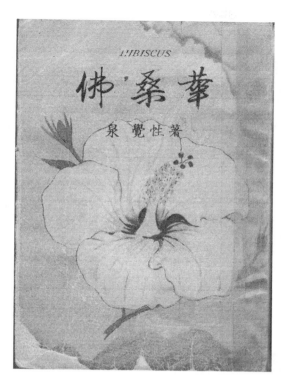

Bussoge

Zoku Bussoge

79

Fundarike

Rev. K. Izumi, Pundarika scroll and Honpa Hongwanji Hawaii Betsuin
taken from a page in "Fundarike

(In his "Bussoge" and "Fundarike" books, are included many of his "Tanka" poems that portray how very human and open-mindedly sincere a person Father was. Among poems he wrote about Mother, there are two poems he wrote about her that tells how he felt about her. I told Mother that there is no greater happiness for a woman to have her husband show how much he loves her by writing it into poetry, that she is a very fortunate woman and wife so loved by her husband.

（十億の女の中に唯一人吾が妻と呼ぼふ縁愛しも）
"Juuoku no onna no naka ni tada hitori
　waga tsuma to yobou enishigana shimo"
Among a billion women, there is only one woman,
I call my wife, who I married and love

（十二人子を持ちながらこの年でなほ妻を愛撫す我を恥じつつ）
"Juuni nin ko wo mochinagara kono toshi de nao
　　tsuma wo ainasu ware wo haji tsutsu"
Even after having 12 children, at my age as I still caress
my wife, I am embarrassed at myself)

(Although having worked until he was 68 years old, when he suffered the first of his 3 strokes, our parents never recovered from the financial hardships that continued after the internment, to buy a home of their own. Father said that he did not have any property to leave to his children but that these 3 books were his inheritance to us. His books are now found in the Hongwanji Betsuin library in Honolulu. He also had the opportunity to place his books in the temples at the altars of Bishop Ekaku Koreyama and Bishop Renshiki Tada, as well as his Izumi parents' altar when he visited Japan years later.)

(In his first book, " Bussoge", published in 1953, in Honolulu, there is a chapter written about the April 1st, 1946, tsunami and how Father had helped to erect the monument for the victims. Since this chapter was written in Japanese, he referred to the tidal wave as tsunami. As the entire book is written in Japanese, not too many younger generations of Japanese today, would be able to read his book. In the translation by daughter, Tomoko, of the chapter on the 1946 tsunami that hit the Hawaiian Islands, particularly, of the disaster it caused at Laupahoehoe High and Elementary School that traumatic morning, will substantiate the fact of Father's resolve to built the tidal wave victims' memorial monument. In Rev. Kakusho Izumi's first book, "Bussoge", I will refer to the "Tsunami", the Japanese word meaning tidal wave as tidal wave, as it was called at that time, and now called universally, Tsunami.)

MEMORIES OF THE TIDAL WAVE

It was the morning of April 1st, 1946. It was around 7:00 a.m., that the first busload of students from the Honohina areas had already reached the Laupahoehoe High and Elementary School on the Big Island of Hawaii. Students from Ookala had also arrived at the school.

As usual, some of the students, when they reached the school, which was located on the sea level ground, went out to the back athletic field to play. The students in the playground, surrounded by the ocean, looked towards the sea, and found that the waves had receded all

81

the way into the sea, showing the black jutting lava rocks. It was such a rare and unusual sight that the young 14, 15-year old boys ran down to the beach. At the moment, the waves that had receded came rushing back to shore, getting bigger and taller like 35 feet and became the terrible tidal wave. About 25 students who were standing on the bleachers were washed away into the sea before one could even utter a word.

There were 4 teachers' cottages built by the County on the school grounds very close to the ocean. The waves had torn the cottages down and there was nothing left but the slabs of concrete where they once stood.

Four teachers from Ohio, Miami and other university graduates were living in the first cottage. Ms. D., Ms. J., Ms. K. and Ms. McGinnis, (beautiful young teachers in their 20s) all became victims of the tidal wave, except for Ms. McGinnis, who was the physical education teacher, survived by hanging onto a door, until she was rescued at around 4:00 p.m. the same afternoon by Dr. L.F., the plantation doctor. The other three teachers' bodies were never found. Mr. K. also became a victim of the tidal wave. Among the teachers of Japanese descent, Mr. N., whose wife had given birth to a baby boy recently, was sitting at the breakfast table drinking his coffee, when he heard the loud noise of the cottage next door breaking down, stood up to go and see what it was, when at that moment, his cottage was demolished by the wave and they were all washed out to sea. Mr. N. lost consciousness but was saved by a student, however, sadly and unfortunately, his wife and three children were all lost at sea. (His eldest daughter was saved.)

I went down to the school grounds amidst all that chaos at around 2:00 p.m. that afternoon. There were water puddles here and there in holes in the grounds and dead fishes lying all over. A phonograph lay broken where the cottage had once stood, children's toys lay there all wet, and grains of rice also scattered here and there.

Involuntarily, the (念仏、南無阿弥陀仏,) "Nembutsu, Namo Amida Butsu," a prayer in Amida Buddha's name, kept flowing out of myself. I chanted the (阿弥陀経,) "Amida kyo," sutra as I walked the desolate grounds of the school, performing the first memorial service for the victims lost on that tragic day.

The months and days have elapsed, and this year will be the 7th memorial anniversary of that unforgettable tragedy. The young students became victims of that tidal wave simply because they reached school early. The young teachers, also became victims, both students and teachers, in just seconds, because they lived in houses on grounds so close to the sea. Among the students that were rescued by Dr. F. were Ronald Yamaoka and Yoshio A.

Young Yamaoka told me, when I visited him in the hospital, that he sank deep to the bottom of the sea when suddenly he was propelled up to the surface as though being pushed up. He floated up right next to a broken piece of lumber, and hung on to that for around 9 hours, when Dr. F saved him. He was never so happy at that moment as when he was rescued. The area where he first sank and was pushed up was where his father had died while he was fishing many years ago. His father's spirit must have saved him and he found himself saying the "Nembutsu." (Ronald is a close friend and classmate of mine and was always a Christian so I think when my father wrote that Ronald prayed by saying the "Nembutsu", it was because the rest of the Yamaokas were all members of our temple.)

Herbert Nishimoto, Takashi T., from Honohina and Asao. K., from Ookala, were hanging on to a roof when a raft was dropped off by a search plane. They climbed onto the raft and were rescued the following morning near the Kohala shores by a kind Hawaiian man after more than 20 hours at sea.

Student M. from Honohina Mauka and Mrs. A. were saved by a military ship and landed at Hilo harbor. How do you all feel about this? Among those that were swept out to sea, seven students, one teacher and one lady survived miraculously from this tragedy. Yet, 24 people became the victims of this tsunami that hit Laupahoehoe Point. Was this what you might call fate, or was this the mysterious ways of the Karma of each person? Herein lies the deep meaning, which is yet to be solved, that we must think about. "Faith or Belief in one's Fate's mysterious ways is a frightening thing", said the founder, (真田まさまる先生,) "Sanada Masamaru Sensei,") a teacher of (仏教再生群,) "Bukkyou Saisei Gun," a group that follows the Buddhism's belief in the reincarnation of life.

However, to tell you the truth, I feel that the realization of the fact, that I was born and am alive today, is in itself, due to the Immeasurable Light and Compassion of the "Amida Buddha" that has embraced and held me close. There is no other way, but to thank and to repent my wrongdoings, by repeating the "Nembutsu," for the very life that I have been given.

My friend, who lost his only child in this tsunami, came to me and cried, "Rev. Izumi, at "O-bon", a Buddhist service to remember and honor those that have passed on, I don't even have a grave for my son where I can pray for him", and shed manly tears for his lost only child. "Oh, that is right. We should have a monument to commemorate those who lost their lives in the name of education at Laupahoehoe School", and at that moment, I made a decision to talk and collect donations from the people from Honohina, Pappaloa, Ookala and the small villages within that area. One year later, a monument was erected and dedicated on the grounds of the school. April 1st has come again and I can still see in my mind's eye, the relatives of the tsunami victims in front of the memorial monument, remembering their lost dear ones.

("合掌,) "Gassho.")

(Gassho means to put your hands together, and repeat the "Nembutsu, Namo Amida Butsu," and all prayers and chants in our Jodo Shinshu services, end with Gassho. Sentences written in the ( ) parenthesis, are what I, Tomoko, wrote down and was not explained in my father's book. Some of the details as to what the survivors were hanging on to may be confused as to what the survivors told him when he visited them at the hospital because there were several of them and Father did not understand English very well. Also, his version of the tsunami was part of a sermon he aired on radio after moving to Honolulu in 1951, as recalled from his memory of the tragedy.)

###

After the tsunami, school was closed until the debris had been cleared, and the damaged buildings had been reconstructed, substitute teachers were found, and classes began again, in a somber atmosphere.

The school year ended, and just before the last days, the new principal had already arrived. Mr. C. called us, the Izumi children, to the office, and after hearing of our education, albeit in Japanese at Crystal City, he told Hiromichi and me to attend summer school at the plantation Manager's home, where the Manager's wife taught English to her children during the summer. He would then let me skip fifth and sixth grades to be in the seventh grade in September when the new school term began. I and Hiromichi would be one grade behind our age level. Takaaki and Junko both were advised to start from the ninth grade, because the lessons taught in the ninth grade and upper grades were too important to miss.

(The years of internment brought on other resentful outcomes. Not being able to finish high school and graduate at our proper ages made us lose all those years and delayed starting to go to college or to university. For some of us sisters, we were not able to seek higher education due to lack of tuition. Going to work right after graduation was alright but if we were to do that anyway, internment did take away some years of time, when we could have been already working and earning wages, to ease the unending financial burdens.)

When school began in September, Takaaki blew the bugle week day mornings before school started for the raising of the flag, and every afternoon for the lowering of the flag. We all went to our assigned grades to begin our days with friends we already knew and to meet new friends. This gave me a feeling of at last belonging, to feel that some worries of having being uprooted by the unexpected events caused by our government, were now finally coming to a sense of ease, falling into some sense of comfortable freedom. Forced to be with students so much younger than myself in the fourth grade last school year, had made me feel a bit resentful of the years of regimented classes at the Crystal City Internment Camp "Kokimin Gakko" Japanese school. Although we had been trained to think like children of Japan, it didn't take long for me to become the outspoken, outgoing American citizen child that I was before the internment.

The first day of school as a seventh grader was an exciting day for me. Although I would be several months to a year older than some of my classmates, since I had spent the last school year from January to June as a fourth grader, it was a nice feeling to be among classmates that were closer to my age. Also, there were classmates whose birthdays were soon after September, when I had a birthday, and so that made me only a month or so older than some of them.

Miwako Miura and Itsuko Kiyota, both from Ookala, became close friends to me almost from the very beginning of our meetings. Miwako was an eye-catching pretty girl with thick pigtails, big twinkling eyes and very personable. Itsuko, more on the quiet side, also had thick pigtails and stood out because she was much taller than us. (It surprised me that she knew she wanted to become a nurse even then and she did, indeed, become one. They were both born five minutes apart on April 15th, fortunately, their homes being close enough for the midwife to attend their births, which was also the same date my mother was born.)

The classmates I already knew were Momoe Ikemoto, Tsuyako Tanaka, Eiko Adachi, Akino Higa, Evelyn Pacaldo, Fujiko Otomo, Florence Pung, Yoso Ishizu, Ronald Yamaoka, George Takeuchi, Jim Terada, Takio Shitabata, Hisashi Hirata and Kenneth Kubo. From the Lauphoehoe area were new friends, Setsuko Shimabukuro, Mabel Une, Violet and Frank De Caires, Margaret Jansen, Stella Cardoza, Wilson Hamasaki, and Wilfred Laeha. The new friends from Ookala were Trinidad Abella, Rosalina Sabella, Ernest Luke, Alvin Sanborn, Frank Kuniyuki, Wallace Nakama, Charles Awazu and Rudy Obiacoro.

The classmates transferring from Ninole and Honohina, Yaeko Matsuda, Doris Fujimoto, Emma Fujimoto, Gloria Tolentino, Tadashi Hirayama, Yoshiaki Sonoda, Koosho Yoza will be enrolling the following year as 8th graders since John M. Ross Elementary School had classes up to the 7th grade. There were others that belonged in our class and I still think of them as part of my Laupahoehoe classmates. (I already knew Irene Tokuda from Sunday school at Honohina Hongwanji where she also played the organ but she joined us as sophomores after attending Intermediate School at Hakalau.)

Ronald Yamaoka became a very good friend as we walked to school, meeting along the way. He was very outspoken and popular and was a cheerleader also. (Ronald will become a leader of our class and a physician specializing in Neurology. He decided on a medical career after being saved by Dr. F in the tragic tsunami that hit Laupahoehoe. He served in the military and retired as a Colonel with a distinguished career as a physician, called to give lectures on his specialty and respected by his fellow colleagues. In one of his tours of duty, he was the Commander of the Medical Military Unit in Camp Zama, Japan and the Surgeon of USARJ (United States Army Japan. Some of the classmates that were invited to his retirement ceremony at the Tripler Army Medical Center Hospital in Honolulu were so proud of him, for we could see how much the people there acknowledged and thought highly of him.)

(I graduated from McKinley High School after attending there for three months of my junior year and my senior year, and have made some close friends from among the several hundreds of classmates there also. I go to the reunions for our class at McKinley and enjoy the friendship from my classmates there too. Perhaps, because of the daily intermingling of family concerns with the 48 Laupahoehoe classmates with whom I shared many years of growing up together into our teenage years to adulthood, I think of Papaaloa in the Laupahoehoe district as my home town instead of Puunene, Maui where I was born, with no recollection of memories spent there.)

(Tsuyako (Tanaka) Fujitani, our alumni secretary-treasurer, and I have had the pleasure and honor of arranging every class reunion for this Laupahoehoe Class of 1952, starting by going back to the Big Island of Hawaii every 5 years since 1957, attending the annual community services for the victims of the 1941 tsunami, a picnic at the pavilion down at the Laupahoehoe Point, ending the three-day reunion with a banquet in Hilo, until we became 65 years old and retired. We then held our annual reunions in Las Vegas and classmates from Hawaii, San Francisco, Oakland, Los Angeles, Oregon, Chicago, New Orleans, Delaware, and Las Vegas, gathered there once every year.

Laupahoehoe 1952 classmates, Las Vegas reunion

We had an especially happy Las Vegas reunion in September, 2015. We were able to find Rudy Obiacoro living in Washington state and we got to meet him after 64 years. The years since we parted flew out of the window and the feeling of friendship was the same as when we were in high school, as though it was only yesterday when we last parted. We enjoyed his wife, Carlene, telling us how they met and she felt just like one of us too, as are all the spouses that have joined us at our reunions. Although I had made all the arrangements for this reunion, I was planning not to go to it because I was to attend the very last Crystal City Internment Camp reunion where the attendees were all internees held confined during World War II and their families in October, a month after our class reunion, Dr. Ronald Yamaoka, the leader of our class, kindly and generously bought me my "Las Vegas package," which enabled me to be there. It was especially gratifying for if not for his generosity, I would have missed meeting Rudy again. Thank you, Ronald, not only for this generous gift, but always, giving me your support every time I needed your help and appropriate advices. Thank you also, for always including me in your family functions and making me feel as a kin and for the friendship we shared since 1946.

(Because our school where we all met is still very important to us, we continued going back to Laupahoehoe every 5th year in April, and again met as usual, in Las Vegas in September. Meeting in Las Vegas brought more classmates together as it is centralized for them to fly there from their homes on the Mainland, and for us to fly there from Hawaii. Many of the Mainland classmates find that it is too expensive to go back to Laupahoehoe with airfare, car rentals, and hotel accommodations for several days. Most of us who live in Honolulu, have relatives that still live in Hilo and Laupahoehoe, that we can stay with and several of us can share the cost of a rented car.)

We have continued to be very close friends, this class of ours, and those of us that live on Oahu, meet at least several times every year also. Friendships developed in our childhood can be of such joy and we can rely on each other without hesitation on any condition or situation, and this feeling is always renewed at our reunions, even as we inevitably lose those that have passed on and remembered as we talk about those good old days of our youth.

Ronald, Tomoko, 7th grade and at 55th reunion at Laupahoehoe

Father and Mother sat Junko and me in the parlor, and we had a discussion on who should have piano lessons, so that one of us could help Father in his ministry work and play the organ for the services. Although Junko had started piano lessons in Kauai, where Father was assigned to the Kilauea Hongwanji, Mother and Junko both said that she should take sewing lessons, and so it was decided that I go to Hilo to learn how to play the piano. These decisions were again an added burden to our already stretched budget, but Father and Mother felt they were necessary. They purchased a second-hand used sewing machine. They could not afford to buy a piano for me to practice at home so Father asked Mr. Ishizu, a staunch supporter of the temple, and a friend (Mr. Ishizu was also originally from Hiroshima,) if he could help us to buy a piano. Mr. Ishizu bought the second-hand piano from Moses Company in Hilo with a large down payment, so that Father's monthly installment payments would be smaller and affordable. (Junko, after graduating from high school, got a job as the secretary to the Plantation Manager, and repaid the deposit for the piano to Mr. Ishizu.)

Junko and I started our assigned lessons. Luckily, Junko learned how to sew from M.H., who lived in Papaaloa, and could walk to her home. (I do not remember seeing Junko sewing at home but she told me when I asked her recently, that she kept the second-hand sewing machine at M.'s residence and sewed our clothes there while she learned how to sew.) From that time on, she sewed all of the children's clothing for many years, even the khaki trousers for our brothers, which must have been more difficult than their shirts. I still remember the gowns she sewed for us to wear at the school proms, happy and proud to wear them, for they were beautifully made from satin and lace. Ready-made clothing was expensive to buy, but she helped in keeping our clothing costs down with all her hard-working sewing.

Three girls who were members of our Sunday school at the temple were going to Hilo for piano lessons, and so I also started my lessons with their teacher, riding to Hilo every Saturday morning on the Yamada Bus from the Laupahoehoe Transport Co. It took an hour and fifteen minutes to reach Hilo in those days, and so I took the 6:30 a.m. bus for my 9:00 a.m. lesson. Once a month I went to the Moses Company to make a payment for the piano. I would then walk on Kilauea Avenue, always passing in front of Hilo Hongwanji, and on to Panawea Street for my lessons. The teacher sat in a chair next to the piano bench on which I sat, and began the lessons with the scale. I was small for my age, and my fingers could hardly span an octave, could not hold my hands in the form taught, and her usual saying to me at each lesson was, "I hear a dying mosquito." An upper class student at our school also took lessons from Mrs. M. and he played the beautiful piece, "Falling Waters" on the piano at the school assemblies. I begged Mrs. M. to teach that music to me but she said it was too advanced for me. (When I moved to Honolulu, I bought the sheet music and practiced stanza by stanza and was so happy when I could play it.)

When my lessons were over, I had to wait for the 1:00 p.m. bus to return home, so in the meantime, I always stopped at an (おかず屋,) "0kazu-ya," Japanese food delicatessen that sold (巻き寿司、)"maki sushi、" rolled sushi in seaweed and "inari sushi" cone sushi, (むすび、)"musubi、" rice ball with many other side dishes. I always bought two "inari sushi," vinegar, salt and sugar mixture stirred in the rice and stuffed in the "aburaage," fried "tofu." soybean curd cake、 cut into cone shape, went to the fish market, then located on Mamo Street, and bought freshly made (天麩羅,) "tempura,", fried fishcake which I still enjoy today. I leisurely ate them on the bus and on the way home, got off at Papaikou Hongwanji Mission for organ lessons from the minister's wife. She taught me from the book of Gathas (Buddhist hymns,) since I had to play the organ for the services as soon as possible. I looked forward to a day off from my laundry duty which was my chore every day after school except on Saturdays. My piano lessons ended after two years, as I could already read musical notes, and Father told me to practice what I had learned now with the Buddhist gathas on the organ. I began playing the organ at the services at the Papaaloa Hongwanji and the Honohina Hongwanji soon after I started my piano and organ lessons. Because there was a shortage of ministers post-war, as some of them had chosen to return to Japan, Father was assigned to the area from Honohina to Ookala to service the members of the Hongwanji Mission. Most of the ministers had to oversee several temples in those times until more ministers came to Hawaii again.

Hiromichi had an ear for music and used to play the piano quite well without even knowing how to read notes. The second-grade teacher, who was the elementary music teacher, Mrs. E.R., recognized his talent and gave him free piano lessons. He could play songs he knew by ear and I used to envy that talent while I labored diligently to practice my scales and lessons every day.

Whenever Hiromichi wanted to play with his friends, Mother would tell me to go with him. He helped by playing with the younger children too.

Hiromichi and Katsuyo in front yard

After the Sunday school services in the morning at Papaaloa Hongwanji, Father and I would drive to Honohina Hongwanji for their services. I played the organ for both services and for the afternoon services for the adults. Irene, my classmate and Joanne F. also played the organ there and we took turns at the Honohina services. Wataru I., a devout member of the congregation was a big help and assistant to Father there.

Once a month, Father would set aside an evening for each village and held a Sunday school service, a YBA (Young Buddhist Association) service, and an adult service for the parents. He did this because many members of the congregation did not own cars and could not come to the temples on Sunday because of the distance.

If one of the homes in the villages had a piano, or at the Kapehu Clubhouse, I would play the piano there but otherwise, Father made me sing one line at a time, and taught the gathas, Buddhist hymns, to the members at each service. There were many teachings of the Buddha in those gathas, both in Japanese and in English.

I recall that on the first Saturday evenings of each month, he went to the village, Honohina Mauka, for these services. This was the only village that I somehow did not go with Father. On one of those Saturday evenings, he did not come home at the usual time. Everyone else was already asleep, when Mother came to the living room where I was reading a book and told me that she was worried because Father had not come home yet. It was after 10:30 p.m. which also made me very anxious, and so I sat down at the living room window where I could see all the car headlights hit the hill before moving on after the curve on the road, which would shine onto the driveway of the garage where Father parked our car. It was after midnight that I finally, definitely saw the headlights of a car, and that the car drove into the garage. I rushed out the door and ran to the garage, where I had left the doors open, and to my utter dismay and fright, the garage was empty. I felt cold all over and was so scared, for then I thought it must be an omen that something terrible must have happened to Father, like falling off the road, which had only a low metal fence at the edge of a cliff, where the ocean waves hit the bottom of the cliff. Because of my ardent prayer and wish for Father to come home, my imagination actually saw the car go into the garage. As it was, there were so few homes that owned cars, so the waiting for the headlights shining on that hill was long in between, before a car drove by. I could not fall asleep that night, because I knew that Father used to call us occasionally from Mr. Y.'s home. It was early the next morning that he called us from Kawahara Garage in Honohina, letting us know that his car would not start, and was towed there. Mr. Y., who was a luna (field manager,) had retired from Hakalau Plantation the month before, and so the telephone in his home had been removed since it had been a work telephone, and Father had no way of letting us know that he would be spending the night at Mr. Y.'s home. Father rode the Hakalau plantation truck that had come to pick up the workers and was able to call us from the garage. He asked us to start the Sunday school and explain why he could not be there, but that he would go to the Honohina Hongwanji and perform the Sunday School service there. (I wrote about this incident in my Senior Year English Literature class assignment when the theme was for a fearful experience that had happened to us. The anxiety and fear for Father's safety that Mother and I went through all night, and the utmost relief we felt when I answered his call the next morning, still remain vividly in my memory.)

It was on the way to and from these services, that I got my oral Japanese language lessons in the car. Father's method of teaching me words and their meanings, was to say it in three different ways of usages, to persons younger than oneself, to one's peers, and in honorific form to elders or persons of high positions. He also taught me words that had the same meanings but said differently, and characters pronounced similarly, but with different meanings. I had to be alert and really learn them for he gave me oral exams on our next outings. (At times, I resented those lessons, not knowing that in the future, they would be the basis of my being able to speak proper Japanese, and qualified me to become a medical translator for Japanese patients that could not speak English at a medical center.)

CHAPTER 8

MEDICAL CENTER IN HONOLULU: CONSULTANT, INTERNATIONAL RELATIONS

During the nearly 12 years working as a Unit Secretary in the Medical Center's Emergency Department, coordinating physicians' and nurses' orders in the 1970s and the 1980s, I also volunteered to translate for the Japanese tourists that came for treatments to the Emergency Department.

I began working at the Medical Center's Human Services department part-time as a file clerk and after a few months there, typed out the "jobs available" flyer and pasted them in the various bulletin boards. There was an opening of a Unit Secretary in the Emergency Department. I always wanted to be a nurse but since I gave up going to college or nursing school, I decided to apply for this job. Fortunately, at this hospital, they hired in-house personnel first before considering applicants from outside.

In my interview with Ms. I., the Emergency Department head, I told her that I had never worked in a hospital, only in offices as a clerk. She then had only one question for me "Do you know any medical terminology?" (19 years ago, I had dated a surgical resident from Japan and instead of the usual dinner or movie dates, we went to the medical library where I copied out of the "Annals of Surgery," surgeries that he had performed. He would tell me the organ in Japanese and the surgical procedure in English and I would write about the organ, write down the procedure, for instance, gall bladder and cholecystectomy, etc.) I replied, "I know what oophorectomy is, resection of the ovary." I was to transfer to the ER the very next Monday, which was the day after Christmas. I was trained for 4 days when I was told that from New Year's day on, I would be "on my own" and if handling one of the busiest days in the ED goes well, thereafter, my orientation was over.

This job was not like the nursing career that I had hoped for in high school but I was very happy to be part of the staff of an Emergency Department, coordinating the doctors' diagnostic tests orders, writing out requisitions, receiving the result of tests by telephone and documenting them to place onto the patients' charts for their treatments. I was very grateful for the kindness of the radiologists, who did not mind teaching me how to spell some of the bones and muscles, words that I had heard for the first time. Answering phone calls, helping to call for supplies needed, calling the attending physicians' offices or the Physicians Exchange when their patients needed admitting, booking a bed with Admitting department, called designated diagnostic departments to schedule tests, calling transporters to take patients to and fro for tests and back to the ED, prioritizing what should be done first for critical patients was mandatory in an ED, having to stabilize patients "STAT!" When the Nurses' Aides were busy with a trauma patient, I even ran up 4 flights of stairs to the laboratory for O-negative blood for transfusions when the elevator would take a while to reach the 1st floor. It was an exciting and a gratifying job to see patients get discharged and some to be admitted to units for continued treatments.

The telemetry equipment in the nurses' station was placed on a shelf in the corner above my desk and the nurses taught me what a PVC looked like, and to alert them if they were with other patients. One can learn a lot, working as a Unit Secretary, calling technicians from the Imaging department for portable X-rays, EKGs from the Cardiac Non-invasive department, Respiratory Therapy department for asthmatic patients, and treatments in the ED, coordinate things so that the 18 rooms could be made ready for the next patient as soon as possible. One never knows what kind of patients would be brought in and every minute counts in critical cases. The busiest 8-hour shift I worked on was to have 64 patients come during that shift, one after the other and sometimes, no time to even take a break or to eat meals. But when patients got discharged or admitted to the units, it felt very worthwhile and relieved, which was to me, the best part of this job.

While still working in the old Emergency Department, I was asked by Dr. Raymond Taniguchi, a respected and highly-skilled brain neurosurgeon, to translate for his Japanese-speaking patients.

Dr. Raymond Taniguchi

In 1989, he arranged to have me become the Consultant, International Relations, until my retirement in 2003. After a forty-hour work weekdays, I was on call by pager 24/7 to come in for translations for Japanese-speaking patients.

For the next 13 years until my retirement in 2003, as I worked as the consultant for international relations, there were many times when I silently thanked Father for those Japanese lessons in the car as we went from villages to villages, to be able to use the proper phrases of words to address the patients, the physicians and medical students who came from Japan for observation externships and after the Kobe earthquake disaster, disaster drills for groups from Emergency Associations. I also coordinated tours for staffs of hospitals, universities, physicians' associations, medical associations, nursing homes personnel, medical residents, students from medical and nursing schools from Japan, China, Taiwan, Korea, Singapore, New Zealand, and even for staffs from some Mainland hospitals. All above work was coordinated with direct supervision of my department head, my mentor, who taught me not only my work in a medical center but also very importantly, human relations. The person that I am today, gratefully, had a lot to having been able to learn and respect her teachings and her "way of life."

Tomoko, Consultant, International Relations

While translating for the Japanese-speaking patients and also when taking the visiting medical groups from Japan on tours, words that I did not even know that I knew, popped out and I silently thanked Father for those oral lessons in Japanese language in the car going from villages to villages that now enabled me to do this work.

The other gratifying part of this work has brought me many friends among co-workers, physicians, staff of the hospital. I met Dr. Steven Nishida, surgeon and Dr. Thomas Kane, III, orthopedic surgeon when they were residents. They would come down to the Emergency Department to admit patients. I knew from the way they cared for their patients and treated them, they would become wonderful attending specialists when they opened their own offices. We became close friends and they are my "adopted sons" for more than 25+ years. They are both successful and well known for their expertise in their fields and their "patient first" kindness. It makes my heart swell with pride when I see them treating the patients and it feels wonderful when Tom calls me, "Mom!" whenever we see each other and I get big hugs in greetings from both him and Steven.

Some of the patients from Japan have become life-long friends. Mr. and Mrs. Gyosai Tamura, famed radio and TV gourmet cooking show star and head of the famous cooking school in Tokyo, have treated me as family and I still enjoy doing things together with Mrs. Tamura for nearly 40 years whenever she comes to Honolulu, The Kishimoto family of Osaka, generations of the owner of Shinrindo, a candy confectionary business, also told me they feel like we are kin for more than twenty years. Chairman and Mrs. Tanabe have sent me New Years greeting cards for more than 30 years, as has Y. Miura. Akira and Sayuri Sato of Hokkaido and Yasuko, from Chiba, also are like my own children for more than 20 years. Hidefumi Ito, who I met more than 30 years ago, won by lottery, permanent residency to the U.S, and bought a home 7 minutes away from my home. Similarly, he and his wife, Mari, are like my children since they treat me like their own mother.

In 2005, Dr. Taniguchi also became the savior of my life by an early diagnosis of a left brain arterial stenosis that he coincidentally found by ordering an MRI/MRA when I complained of sounds of gushing water in my ears. Dr. Taniguchi had his close friend and colleague, Dr. Takanori Fukushima, an internationally famed and noted brain neurosurgeon, known for "his hands, a gift from God," from Raleigh, North Carolina, to come to Hawaii as a consultant. I knew Dr. Fukushima through Dr. Taniguchi and had met him many times when he came to Honolulu and also at the neurosurgical conferences Dr. Taniguchi invited me to. He also got a neurologist, and a radiologist as consultants for my case. I was honored to have Dr. Fukushima examine me in Dr. Taniguchi's office. I was told that the left brain arterial blockage was severe and at my age of 72, with my diagnosis of diabetes mellitus, hypertension and hypercholesterolemia and a history of cardiac arrest, revived by CPR 35 years ago, surgery was too big a risk, and that I was in danger of an imminent CVA (stroke). Dr. Fukushima advised me to be treated aggressively with medications. The site of the blockage was bad and the surgery would take too long. Otherwise, if I were twenty years younger, he would have taken me to Raleigh, N.C. and did the surgery himself. His advice and the treatments by the neurologist prevented a stroke. (I was not surprised to hear my diagnosis for my maternal grandparents, parents, Father's two brothers and my two brothers had suffered strokes, so I thought, now it was my turn since cardiovascular diseases are inherited.)

After a year and a half of treatments of prescribed, aggressive medications, blood tests, 4Life Research's all-natural ingredients and diagnosis-targeted supplemental products that support educate, balance and elevate the immune system functions, 2 more MRI/MRAs, after 1 ½ year, there was enough blood flow through the blockages. The imminent stroke had been prevented, gratefully, by the neurological treatments.

I am gratefully still well today, 10 years after being diagnosed with left brain arterial stenosis. My wholehearted appreciation and gratefulness to Dr. Taniguchi, Dr. Fukushima and the neurologist for preventing the imminent stroke, which was life threatening.

Dr. Takanori Fukushima, Dr. Raymond Taniguchi, Neurosurgeons

To Dr. Taniguchi, who has assisted me in publishing this book goes my heartfelt appreciation and thankfulness, for he has always played a big and irreplaceable role in my life.

With heartfelt gratitude and appreciation, I would like to thank Mr. Kunio Masuko, President of Academy Publishing Co., Ltd. In Tokyo, Japan, as told to me by Dr. Taniguchi, for his important advices regarding my Japanese version of this book.

CHAPTER 9

BACK TO THE YEARS OF CONTINUED HARDSHIPS: PAPAALOA IN THE LAUPAHOEHOE DISTRICT

Not to mention the worries and hardships our parents and older siblings suffered after returning from the Internment Camp, having to do the laundry by hand, since we could not afford to buy a washing machine for more than several years, was my hardship.

There were always diapers to be washed, thoroughly rinsed until the water was clear, so that the baby would not get diaper rash, and then the daily clothing washings. On top of that, in order for the sheets to be really white (there were only white sheets in those days,) they needed to be boiled with soap suds in a big tub filled with water on the kerosene stove, using two burners. We could not afford powdered detergent and so I scraped the brown soap bar into slivers to make suds and boiled the sheets and pillow cases. Once a week, standing on a chair, using a fat guava branch to stir the bed linens, and plopping them into a bucket, carrying the heavy, wet load down to the laundry room that was next to the bathroom with the "furo", I started my days of difficult bed linen washing, unlike my daily laundry washing. The sheets and pillow cases had to be soaped with the same brown soap, moving them a little at a time onto the wooden, corrugated washboard, and scrubbed with a stiff brush until the entire sheet had been scrubbed. It was a very time-consuming chore to wash the sheets in sections until it had been completely scrubbed. Rinsing the laundry more than four times, draining the water from the two tubs and filling them to rinse out the suds were already hard, but the more difficult part of this chore was to wring the water out of the heavy sheets with my little hands, before hanging them up on the clothesline to dry. I wanted to complain that the work was too hard for a 12-year old and so I sang while I worked. This had a dual purpose, as one cannot complain while singing, and while singing, my feelings of complaints and hardships somewhat flew out of the window, and made my work a bit easier.

Father's white dress shirts had to be boiled also before washing, rinsed with bluing to make them look whiter after washing, soaking them in the starch and water that had to be cooked on the stove, and sifted through a cheese cloth so that it would not be lumpy, which made the shirts when dried, stiff and hard. They had to be sprinkled with water and dampened before ironing them. These dress shirts had to be ironed in such a way so as to not have more than one straight line on the sleeves, and had to be dampened over and over until that was achieved. Ironing one side of the sleeve and turning it over to the other side made me make, at times, double lines on the sleeves, and had to be redone. The gas iron was so heavy, it tired me out. Mother praising me that Father loved the way I ironed his dress shirts, made me try even harder to do a good job.

There were older girls that treated me like their little sister. Momo's sisters, H. and C. babysat the younger siblings and were kind to me every time I played with Momo. Since Mother taught Japanese school as well as having her duties as she did at all the other temples, S.S. who helped us before the war, also came again to help with chores. She and her husband, H.N. occasionally, used to take us for rides to Parker Ranch when they went to visit her brother there. A.A., another classmate's older sister who was a seamstress, also was very good to me. I used to walk to their home and sit next to her as she sewed. We chatted while she worked to finish her sewing. I liked looking at her, at times, quietly, for she was very attractive and kind. Y.Y., also a seamstress from another family, was very kind and seemed happy to have me visit her so I went to her home a lot. (I still see her occasionally at the temple in Honolulu, and she must be close to ninety since I am already 82.) Her neighbor, M.H., who lived in the house next to the Y's home, used to give me some of her dresses that she had outgrown. These dresses, the ones that Junko sewed for me, and her hand-me-down dresses, were enjoyed and I proudly wore them. It helped with the finances too. Mother always used to say that to wear clothes that were patched was not shameful as long as they were clean and not smelly. I do not recall that any one of us had to wear patched clothes, so that was only a way that Mother was teaching us to be grateful for whatever we have. Somehow, from the time I was at Crystal City Internment Camp, I was liked by girls much older than me. Betty Uchima. was only few years older, and the youngest among the "big sisters" that I used to visit and chat with. They were all very nice to me and I have fond memories of our visits during the years we lived in Papaaloa.

Maybe because Mother did not have the money for me to perm my hair, I wore my hair straight until my freshman year. When I was 16 and a sophomore in high school, I had my first perm. Now that we were in high school, many of my friends in my class started to use lipstick. They look so attractive that I wanted to put on lipstick too, but Mother forbade me to, saying that I should only be interested in my studies, and not how I look.

I, sometimes slept overnight at another congregation member, M's home in Maulua. Their daughter, K., who was several years older than me, treated me like a younger sister too. When I told her that I wanted to use lipstick but was not allowed to, she gave me a Revlon lipstick, Windsor, which had a pretty, pick-colored hue. Joyfully, I used to hide and use it while I was doing the laundry, set the small mirror that always came with a purse in those days against the wall above the wash basins, looking at myself, and sang while I did the four rinses. Of course, whenever I heard footsteps nearby, I quickly wiped the lipstick off, and tried to look so innocently. This too, made my laundry chore easier. (It was during those hardship years that I discovered, just as Father taught us, that happiness was something one had to make for oneself, and not depend on others to make you happy. It was solely dependent on how you accepted things that happened to you and how you responded to those things.)

When Father finally bought me a washing machine, it was one that only had a wash cycle, and so the same rinsing over and over still continued. There was one consolation because it had a roller which squeezed out the soapy water after the washes, and so the first rinsing was not as soapy as before. Also, after the rinsings, putting the lid back on the machine and using the roller backward, the dampness was much less than wringing the wet laundry with my hands, and the wet laundry lighter in weight, so that was a big help in hanging the clothes up on the high lines to dry.

The clothes dried faster too, because of the wringing out the water after the rinsings. One may not realize until it happened, but before the machine, the laundry was very heavy with the dampness that could not be removed by wringing the water out by hands. Folding the diapers and other clothing that did not need ironing also took a lot of time.

I enjoyed reading and so when the story was interesting and I did not want put the book down, I even read while doing the laundry. One day, as I read while the machine was doing the wash and kept on reading by propping the book against the short wall below the windows above the two wash basins while I did the rinses, when I was squeezing the water out of the clothes as I continued to read, my left arm went into the roller with the clothes. In spite of the fact that I quickly slapped the lever to open the roller, my arm was blistered as though it had been burnt. Father did not scold me and did not tell Mother that I was reading. He sterilized a needle and gave the rather large blisters a tiny prick, cleared the fluid from them, applied a soothing balm and bandaged the arm.

To have learned another lesson the hard way, needless to say, thereafter, I put the book down when using the roller to squeeze out the water from the laundry items.

It took about 40 minutes to wash a load, and so after starting the first load, I usually ran away to play either with Momo or with Florence P. Florence, another classmate, was a wonderful cook, and she always cooked the meals and desserts for her 3 older, handsome brothers. She was amazing, for she baked cookies and cakes without measuring the ingredients, and mixed the batter so matter of factly, it was in awe that I used to see the finished pastries looking so delicious, and done right. She also liked to make me a snack of sandwiches, which we ate together. She was innovative and I ate sandwiches that I didn't make at home. I ate my first deviled ham sandwich at her home. At times, my younger sister, Norie, had to come to find me, and always said the same thing when she did, "Mama said to come home." I had to find my own fun, and did so to relieve the toil of the many household, hard works usually needed to be done in any family.

I think it was about this time that Mother started to say to us, and perhaps, particularly to me, who loved to run away to play quite often, the adage, (心ここにあらざれば、視れども見えず、聴けども聞こえず、食えどもその味を知らず、) "Kokoro koko ni arazareba, mie domo miezu, kike domo kikoezu、kue domo sono aji wo shirazu." If you do not do things wholeheartedly, you see, but you don't see, you hear, but you don't hear, you eat, but you don't taste what you are eating. When we did things halfheartedly and things got done "slipshodly" or with mistakes, she quoted this saying countless times: Do things wholeheartedly and willingly if you are going to do them.

(陰日向無く、) "Kage hinata naku," whether in the shade or in the sunlight, which literally meant when you do things, whether you are being watched or not, do your best diligently and properly. For Mother, this saying also applied to being honest, also to not steal things when you think no one is watching. Mother always said she hated those two things the most, lying and stealing.

The following three sayings were part of the lyrics of one of Mother's favorite songs, (金剛石・水は器、) "Kongo seki ・ MIzu wa utsuwa," titled, "Diamond・Water when in a Vessel," which she learned in school. She wanted us to learn these teachings and repeatedly said them to us.

(金剛石も磨かずば、玉の光は添わざらん、) "Kongoseki mo migakazu ba, Tama no hikari ha sowazaraun," a diamond, also if not polished, its stone will not shine or sparkle, meaning accomplishments can not be met as expected, if effort and endeavor are not put forth.

(人も学びて後にこそ、まことの徳は現るれ、) "Hito mo manabite nochi ni koso, makoto no toku wa arawarure," just as a diamond needs to be polished in order to shine, after you have studied, learned and gained knowledge, you will become a person with sincere truth of highest virtue and morality.

(光蔭惜しみて励みなば、如何なる業かならざらん、) "Hikage oshimite hageminaba, ikanaru waza ka narazaraun," Whether in light or in shade, if you strive and endeavor ungrudgingly, and unsparingly, day and night, in other words, at all times, if you don't begrudge the time spent striving for goals, there is not any art, work, act or deed, or things you will not be able to achieve. (All of these teachings are what the teachers teach when you study "Shushin," Morals and Ethics at Japanese schools.)

Although she was four years younger than me, Florence, Toshie A. used to come over to our home, and I also played with her at her home. Her father was an engineer in the mill, and they lived behind the Plantation store and post office, on the road leading to the mill. He also served as president of the temple. There was a gulch between our homes, the lower flow of Egusa Pond that led to the sea. They raised pigs and her brother would come to collect the slop which was gathered in a can under the palm tree. We were warned not to put any ginger in the slop, so it had to be sorted out. Florence was like another little sister and we got along well. (Our friendship will continue again in Honolulu after she moved there and even after we had both married and had children.)

When we moved to Papaaloa from Kilauea, Hiromichi and I on some nights, slept overnight at the Ishizus. They lived in Kapehu then but, upon our return to Papaaloa after our internment, they now lived in the area close to the hospital, having moved from the plantation house in Kapehu to their own home. Hiromichi and I enjoyed going to the Ishizus. He played with Hachiro (Hatch), who was also his age and I played with Shigeko, who was my age. Even after nearly 4 years apart, because we used to sleep over at their home before the war began, we were very comfortable in their new home across from the Catholic cathedral, near the Terada Soda Works and Terada Bakery. We were treated like family members and I especially enjoyed Mrs. Ishizu's dish of beef cooked in sugar, "shoyu" with potato, carrots and onion.

I had tonsillectomy at the Kilauea Plantation Hospital when I was six or seven years old, as did Junko. The doctor there cut off our uvula when removing our tonsils. By the time I was 13 years old, the tonsil on the right side of my throat had grown again and had gotten bigger until it was near the middle of my throat. Dr. F. was quite surprised to see my uvula gone but said that since I was already talking at the time the first surgery was performed, I could still speak and be heard in a proper voice.

As Father drove me to the plantation hospital for my tonsillectomy that summer day, he preached to me in a gentle, kind manner, that sometimes patients do not regain consciousness from the anesthetic, Ether, and passes away without awakening. He told me to repeat the "Nembutsu" until the ether took effect and to not worry for should that happen, I would be reborn into the Pure Land of Nirvana and be One with Amida Buddha. Having always to obey and follow what our parents told us, I was not afraid, but was looking forward to eat the ice cold, soothing, popsicles that Mother fed us after our tonsillectomy.

At a sugar plantation, one of the jobs is hoe hana (Hawaiian for hoeing the weeds work). The truck would pick up the workers at various spots near the camps early in the morning and take them to the cane fields. Everyone wore long sleeve shirts, and straw hats to work out in the sun, in the cane fields without any trees or shades. In the late afternoon, they would be dropped off again by the truck that went to gather the workers from the various fields.

Before the cane is harvested, the field is set on fire to burn off the leaves, leaving only the cane, which is cut by laborers that wielded flat, wide and about nearly 2 feet long "cut-cane knife" with a wooden handle. The blade had a hook at the end of it that was used to pull the cane closer towards the worker, hold it in one hand as he chopped the long roundish cane into shorter sizes. When the blazes tinted the sky orange with black ashes flying around in the wind, we knew that the harvesting of the canes would be soon in that field. There were many fields so the workers could do their designated jobs all year round.

Large Kenworth trucks hauled the harvested canes to the mill, but there were also flumes, with water running in them, to carry the canes that were cut into shorter sizes with a "cut cane knife," as we used to call those one-sided flat blades with a hook on the front end with wooden handles. The flumes were built on stilts, and started in the fields. The canes thrown in them ended into the grinder as it reached the mill. The flume in the back of our home was built high above the ground, and those had boards running along one side of them so people could walk on them, and push apart the stacks of cane that had gotten stuck and piled up. We used to climb up the supporting boards, jump into the flumes and slide quite a distance in it without even stopping to think of the danger, with the grinder being at the end of the destination. We sometimes, also, took a cane out of the flume, bit the edge of it with our teeth, to pull off the hard outer peel to expose the white cane, and with each bite, chewed and drank the sweet, sugary fluid from it, spat out the flattened remains of the once, round, cane.

I must have been quite a rascal and although I did obey Mother mostly all of the time, my mind was always on how I could have fun. The veranda, right outside of the front door leading to the parlor, had some areas where several slats of wood had rotted from the rain. The carpenters had removed several planks of lumber and we were all reminded by Mother not to go out from that entrance. The wooden door that was usually kept open since there was also a screen door on the inside of that door, on that day, both doors had been closed by Mother. Of course, in my hurry to go out and play, without even thinking why the doors were closed, I promptly opened both doors and stepped out. Too late to remember Mother's warning, to my regretful surprise, I found myself falling the distance of one floor to the ground area, right below where the clothes lines that were used when it rained, were hung. Luckily, the distance of my fall was shortened as I fell onto the piled up chopped wood that the Women's Club of the temple used when cooking on the Hibachi (charcoal grill,) so I got away with abrasions, bruises but no fractures. This time, I did get scolded by Mother, for not heeding and listening to her warnings, as she treated my minor injuries of scraped knees and elbows. (We used to call them strawberries, the red blood and bruises and the coagulated streaks of blood that had turned black resembled strawberries.)

Aa and Pahoehoe in Hawaiian are names of the two types of lava, Lau, in Hawaiian is leaf, thus, Laupahoehoe means Leaf of Lava. Laupahoehoe School was a small school with a small student body and everyone knew each other, or at least, which family one belonged to, and which village one came from. It had a friendly atmosphere and the lunches served there were tasty and delicious. My favorite lunches were Spanish rice, Dinner in a Dish and Stuffed cabbage.

I walked pass the stone wall into the front grounds of the school, there was a big Banyan tree, its branches full of leaves reaching outward, and its many roots that were long, and growing outside of the entire bark of the tree. Looking at the front of the school building from where the Banyan tree stood, with the doors to the classrooms and veranda facing the Banyan tree, the flagpole nearby the tree, and the music classroom built in a separated building at the corner end of the school, its door facing the side of the tree, it made it into a U-shaped school, looking at it from the front grounds, but in reality the building was H-shaped. Towards the back athletic field, on the right side, the cafeteria and home economics classroom were adjoined to the classrooms by a veranda, with the shop classroom built under those rooms, on the left side, the fifth and sixth grade classrooms beyond the fourth grade room, unseen from the front grounds facing the school building. The typing, shorthand and bookkeeping rooms started along the front veranda, followed by the dispensary, the library and the principal's office and office staff's room, the science room the last with the middle and high school rooms starting from that corner, Beyond the stone wall enclosing the front grounds and across the paved road, was the gymnasium.

One afternoon, just as I was walking past the side of the music room building to go home, I stepped on a big brown centipede and got stung on my right little toe. There were two red blood puncture holes there and, although the toe did not swell, it was very painful. I was crying softly as I walked up the hill and decided to stop at the hospital on the way home. To my surprise, as I neared the hospital, without even noticing it, the pain was gone. Since there was no swelling, it seemed as though I had not been stung at all except for the two puncture holes left by the centipede bite. The long walk uphill and the circulation of the blood was all the treatment it needed. Most of the students, except for a few, went to school barefooted.

Walking the long distance to school and back home every day, one of the things I looked forward to, was the clean spring water coming out of pipes from the hillside between the last housing area in Puulai, and the starting of the narrow road leading downhill towards the school. I always stopped to drink the continuously-flowing, clear, naturally cold, and delicious water from those pipes. Walking uphill until almost reaching Puulai, the after school weather being warmer than in the early morning walks to school, the cold water tasted even better.

I think it may have been when we were eighth graders, Mrs. T., the music teacher, put on an operetta called, "Love Pirates of Hawaii," on the stage in the gymnasium, and the cast was chosen from the entire student body. Some of the boys, with black patches over one eye, moustaches and beards drawn on their faces with charcoal made great pirates. Girls from various classes wore white dresses with blossoms in their hair with makeup on (I and other classmates were among the girls,) the lead stars were the pirate Captain, an Admiral of the Navy, looking so handsome and tall in his white suit uniform and hat, and the female star dressed in a gown. My "hanai sister," Kawaihona was cast as the supporting female role. I can't remember any of the songs we sang, except for one that was sung by the female star and we sang the chorus together.

Aloha
"In fair Hawaii, there's one word you should know
For you'll find it everywhere, no matter where you go
It has meanings many, it's when you say it and how
If you'll listen carefully, I'll tell it to you now......

When you wish to greet a friend, simply say, Aloha
To your sweetheart you would sing, sweetly, softly, Aloha
And at parting, leis you bring, and good wishes, Aloha."

It was one of the highlights of that school year and was enjoyed by everyone, even parents came to see it.

We had a sort of craft fair and I remember a Hawaiian band came from Hilo and sang. The operetta was the finale of the event.

Upon arriving home from school, before doing the laundry, I did the marketing. Since the members of the congregation had gardens with vegetables, many of them would bring the first crop of eggplant, turnip, green onion, carrot, radish, lettuce, tomato, pumpkin, string bean, etc. to give to us, and so I only bought rice, potatoes, onion, cabbage, meats, and other necessities from the Plantation Store, bread from Tabata Store and Yamanouchi Store, alternating between the two owners since both were members of our temple. Sometimes, eggs were given by members that raised chickens and once in a while, even a live chicken, which I had to prepare.

While on my errand to the stores, at times, I dared to ask Mother if I could buy a candy bar, Butterfinger being my favorite, and to my joy, she would give me coins to buy it. However, she would say to me, "Tomo-chan, (a form of endearment) if you bring the candy home and cut it into two pieces, two of you can enjoy it, if you cut it into four pieces, four of you can enjoy it, but if you cut it into bite-size pieces, all of you can enjoy it. If you don't wish to share it, eat it before you come home." There were more times when I brought the candy bar home, but at times, gave in to the temptation and guiltily ate it all by myself. Otherwise, I would buy a Long John pastry or a Custard Danish, as an excuse to enjoy it alone. Terada Bakery in Laupahoehoe, made very delicious pastries, and I can still remember the taste of their Long John, custard Danish and coconut turnover, which were my favorite pastries. (When I became older, I realized that this was Mother's way to teach me to share things and also to learn to be a giving person, not be greedy.)

There was another small store, Sugikawa Store, but they sold canned goods and candy, nothing perishable and so I bought all 3 Libby brand Vienna Sausages, Deviled Ham, Corned Beef, from there. Their youngest son, S., was a close friend of Takaaki, and their daughter, S., was my friend.

A Japanese man, Mr. S., from Hilo, would come once a week, and park his truck right outside of the temple gate, next to the tall pine tree, He had a refrigerator built in the back bed of the truck, filled with fish, and other seafood. Fish was very reasonable then, and other than buying （鰹、） "Katsuo," bonito for (刺身,) " s ashimi," sliced raw fish, for special occasions, Mother bought （鮪） " Maguro、 " tuna, which was more expensive. We also used to buy Opelu (Hawaiian fish) for each one of us. Cleaning the fish, descaling them and many times poking my fingers with the sharp fins or bones was not a pleasant chore. Although Opelu has many tiny bones, frying it crisp with salt and pepper, coated lightly with flour, was delicious and we enjoyed eating it.

Junko did most of the cooking but I also cooked dinner once in a while. One of the meals I used to cook was pork sautéed with ginger, round onion, green onion, canned (松茸,) "Matsutake," Japanese mushroom, and long rice, in shoyu and sugar. (As "Matsutake" became very expensive, canned "Matsutake" was no longer imported for years now and I have not been able to see them on the shelves of Asian food sections anywhere.) Across the street from the temple and our home, lived four Japanese families and members of our congregation. One evening, E.F., who lived in one of the houses with her father, invited me to eat this dish. It was delicious and I promptly cooked it for the family the next evening, which was a great hit.

Father and Mother also taught the one-hour Japanese School classes after English school and two-hour classes on Saturday, so Mother was always busy with her work with the temple as well as being a teacher. Ministers were teachers and so they both always taught Japanese at every temple father was assigned to. (This work will always be remembered perpetually because several years ago, when my niece, Kiyomi Shiosaki and her family, visited the Japanese American Cultural Museum in Los Angeles, she saw on the wall a photograph of a Japanese School graduation class from Kilauea, Kauai. In this picture, she recognized her grandparents, our Father and Mother, with the notation of the graduating class photograph sent in by a student in that last 1941 graduation before the war.)

Kilauea Japanese School Graduating Class of 1941

Our brother, Thomas Michio, was born on March 2, 1947, in the car on the way to Matayoshi Hospital in Hilo. The M. family from another temple had befriended Father, and Mrs. M., a nurse, said she would do private-duty nursing for Mother, and for her to give birth at the hospital in Hilo. Mother did not have any birth labor contractions, and her babies gushed out together with the amniotic fluid when her water bag broke. She always had to rush to the hospital when she had her show. Riding all that distance to Hilo, with Father driving and Junko in attendance, she gave birth to Tommy, as he was called, just as they reached Hilo, but not before arriving at the hospital. Father named him Thomas after Thomas Edison, and Michio with the Japanese character (道,) "michi," which means road, (雄,) "o,“) often used in a man's name, and can also be pronounced as "yu," meaning to contend for supremacy, after a renowned Buddhist teacher and author, Izumi, Michio, (whose name was written with the same characters) whom he respected and admired. (I always thought how appropriately named Michio was since he was born on a roadside in the car and for Father to respect a Buddhist teacher and scholar by that very name.)

Tommy was a very smart two years old, and could recite the sutras we prayed together with Father every morning and evening, before the home altar. When our neighbor from across the street offered to babysit him one day, even as a two-year old, he must have known how to come home, for he was crossing the street alone, when he was struck by a limousine-sized bus from Paauilo, and sustained a head injury, cranial skull fracture. Dr. F. did an eight-hour surgery and saved his life. (Tommy had a gap on his frontal skull where the bone did not merge as he grew older into adulthood.)

Another frightening incident was when he fell from the height of two floors, out of the screen of the opened kitchen window, by standing up on his high chair, which shouldn't have been placed next to the window. His weight took the screen off as he fell against it. Luckily, as we all ran down sobbing with our hearts in our throats, the laundry line probably saved his life, for several of them were broken, and must have brought him down slowly. He did not even have a scratch on him nor seemed to have fallen on his head. He was not even crying as we grabbed and carried him from the rectangular screen he was still on and hugged him. All of us ran down barefooted and was crying but he was alright falling onto the lawn. What a frightening feeling it was, to see him fall out of the window, horror and coldness and dread enveloping us, he being there one minute, and gone the next. It happened so suddenly, it was a shocking experience, to say the least.

Father with Tommy and Mother with Tommy

Katsuyo with Tommy

Duane, our youngest brother, was born at home. We were already a family of 9 siblings, 5 daughters and 4 sons. It is important in a Japanese family, to have sons to carry on the family name. Father's friend and minister at the Hongwanji, came over soon after Tommy was born, and pleaded with our parents that in the event that they might have another child, would they consider having a doctor of Japanese ancestry, who owned a hospital, adopt the baby. He assured them that the doctor was a very good person, but had no children or relatives to take over the hospital. He wanted to adopt a child from a good family, to be his heir, and promised to educate him or her to become a physician, and to inherit the hospital. After thinking it over and over, at a time when they were still trying to recoup our financial situation after coming back from Crystal City, and having all of us children, our parents agreed to give the next baby up for adoption, also thinking that the child may be able to have better opportunities in life, and to become a doctor. They felt sympathy for the doctor and his wife and thought how sad they must be, to not be blessed with children, for they always said that their children were their treasures.

Mother did get pregnant again. Rev. T. had been notified of her pregnancy, and she was to deliver the baby at the hospital. On the morning of February 28, 1949, as we were getting ready to go to school, and Father was in the temple for his daily morning prayer, Mother told me to call him because she had a show. The ride to the hospital in Honokaa was a distance close to around a two-hour or more drive away. I went to the temple to call Father and when he was rushing to get ready, Mother said that it was too late, and that she feels like the baby would be born soon. Father asked Junko to come and attend to Mother, for me to

110

call Dr. F. to come for a house call visit. As I was dialing his number, I heard the baby crying and so this time, she had given birth at home. The rest of the siblings were in the other bedroom. Dr. F came, and after cutting the umbilical cord, examined both mother and the new baby son. He did not believe that Mother had no birth contractions so warned her that should she have another child, not to wait, but to come to the hospital right after she had a show.

The baby was a cute, strong-looking boy, with rings around his ankles and wrists, with a solid feel when we held his arms and legs.

Mother cuddled him and kept looking at his face, not saying a word. Father also kept looking at the baby but not saying a word. Junko and I carried the baby and wanted to say that we should not give him away but the words could not be uttered. As we gathered around the newborn, the atmosphere in the room was sad, dark and heavy, and even seemed painful. As we siblings looked at each other, we silently decided and agreed we could not give our new baby away. Everyone's faces lit up and we started to laugh aloud, elated.

Father promptly called Rev. T. and explaining the situation, apologized profusely and told him that we had decided that we could not give the baby up for adoption. Rev. T. understood as he was a father of an only child, W.A., who was the same age as Hiromichi and they had played together in camp. Father asked him to apologize and explain everything to the doctor. Junko named the new baby, Duane, and Father named him Satoru, using the character, (覚,) "kaku," meaning enlightened from part of his name (覚性,) "Kakusho," and the character "Kaku" also could be read as Satoru.

One can imagine how difficult and heartbreaking it is to give up one's child, and it would probably have been easier to have given birth at the hospital, and left Duane there, but having seen him and cuddled him, even the thought of giving him up was very painful. Our family was thankful to keep our new son and brother.)

Father with Duane

It was the night of November 30, 1950, around 8:30 p.m., when I had been visiting Fujiko, my classmate, I was told to come home because Mother had to go to the hospital to have another baby. This was to be her 12th and last child. Although she did go in early as suggested by Dr. F. when Duane was born, she gave birth after midnight, and so by the time he was called by the nurse, and came to the hospital from his home on the hospital grounds, the baby was already born. The nurse had witnessed that Mother, indeed, did not have any birth contractions and as usual, the baby simply was born when her water bag broke. Dr. F. decided to do tubal ligation sterilization surgery to prevent further pregnancies, and at the same time performed an appendectomy on Mother. I did not have an English name, being born two years after our parents arrived in Hawaii and did not speak any English. This never bothered me, for many children born in Hawaii from immigrant families in those days, mostly did not have English names. I always thought the name Ann or Anne was pretty but when I heard the name Anna, I just loved it. This time, I named the new baby sister, Anna, and Junko named her Takeko after (九条武子夫人,) "Kujo Takeko Fujin." Junko had read a book on Buddhism written by Lady Kujo at age 16 and respected and admired her since. On December 1st, 1950, we all welcomed Anna, our littlest sister. She was an adorable baby, big eyes, with very fair complexion, and her hair had a light-red hue to it. We all loved her and enjoyed taking care of her.

As usual, whenever Mother gave birth to a new baby, small in stature that she was, she had ample breast milk and had breast fed all of us for a whole year. When she fed the new baby, we siblings would stand in a row, and after the baby was fed, she would squeeze her breast and shoot her milk into our mouths. We must have looked like baby birds with our mouths wide open to receive the warm and very sweet milk. This was a ritual which we older siblings enjoyed, just a spray of Mother's milk, filled with her love for her children.

I had to babysit my younger siblings, and the once-a-month well-baby examinations at the Papaaloa gymnasium by Dr. F., was also my responsibility. Dr. F. used to tease me, as I was the only sister with the new infant there among the mothers, and so when it was our turn, he would call out, "Grandma Izumi." When Tommy, Duane and Anna became a year old, because I was the one who heard the doctor's instructions on how to make the formula for the milk, which was made from Carnation cream diluted with water, filling them in the milk bottles that had to be sterilized, it became my chore to make the milk with Karo syrup, and baby food for the youngest one. Scraping apple and squeezing them in cheesecloth to make apple juice, mixing the Pablum for their cereal, feeding the baby siblings made me a "maternal" person from a young age.

Anna was only 3 months old when we moved to Honolulu, so I took care of feeding her until she became 1-year old. I was secretly happy when the babies started to eat table food. While tending them, I daydreamed, that someday I would be married, and taking care of my own children. My husband's face was always a blank but, of course, taller than me.

I loved to read the "I Love Betsy" series, mysteries, and as a teenager, books about Julian, an American who married Tabitha, a girl from an English family that settled in Virginia. Many books the author wrote about the generations of that family were my favorite books. I also enjoyed books on early Westerns and somehow felt an affinity to the American Indians. I used to hide under the blanket with a flashlight at bedtime, reading after the lights were out since we children shared one room with thick futons on the floor as our beds. Junko used to do this also. With hardly any time to study, I used to memorize what I crammed the night before a test, and got good grades in the tests with not much studying.

We had a custom of enjoying (おやつ,) "Oyatsu," afternoon snacks. Mother would serve us (饅頭,) "Manju," bean jam bun, coffee candy, Hershey chocolate kisses candy, both individually wrapped, apples and oranges which were the offerings for the altar from members when they held family memorial services at the temple. I still do not like "Manju" after eating it so often. Mother gave the coffee candy to the older children and the chocolate candy to the younger siblings, which was the right thing to do since coffee candy has caffeine in it. (I was not happy about getting coffee candy most of the time, and perhaps my distaste for them and their aroma from those days, made me not drink coffee all of my life. On the other hand, my wanting the Hershey chocolate kisses and not allowed to have them, made me love chocolate in any form all my life.)

Movies were shown in the Papaaloa Theater, across from the Okamura Store, and next to the Ikemoto home. The movie would be shown for only one night, and then sent to the next theater, which was in Ookala. Scenes cut out of movie magazines were pasted on the door, and I would choose the movie I wanted to see, for we were allowed to go to the movies only once a month. Telling Mother, the date of the movie I chose, I looked forward to seeing it with my classmates, Momo and from Kihalani village nearby, Tsuyako, Eiko, Akino, Evelyn. I had told them at school that I would be joining them at the theater. Upon reaching home, rushing to remind Mother that it was my night at the movies, before I could say a word, she would inform me that there were two memorial services that night, and I was to serve tea and cookies to the families after the services, which was another one of my duties. Since we were taught not to talk back to our parents, I would go down to the laundry room in tears. When Father came for his bath, I would tearfully complain to him from the laundry room next to the bath room where the ceiling was open above the wall dividing the two rooms. He always comforted me by saying, "Please understand and help your mother. She has many children, 10 (actually 11 but eldest sister, Megumi, lived in Japan,) of you and many chores herself, so she has to be the disciplinarian." Unfortunately, the next day, my movie moved on to Ookala Theater, and I missed seeing the movie of my choice.

Although it may seem like a trivial matter, the once-a-month movie going, was still part of the hardship of trying to recover unsuccessfully from the financial difficulties suffered from those long years of internment, when Father and Mother had not earned any income during the war. Mother knew that to deprive us from going to the movies would make us unhappy, and I know that she would have loved to be able to do and let us buy whatever we wanted, but just did not have the means to do it. Her already tight budget also included our going to the movies. The younger siblings were also allowed once a month to go to the matinee, and I had to accompany them to watch movies like, "The Green Hornet," "Batman," "Superman," and other super heroes with cartoons before the main show like, "Don Winslow of the Navy".

Many times, I felt some of the things I had to do were unfair, and not being able to explain to Mother how I felt, made me feel resentful. Mother did not allow any back talk from us and the moment I said, "But, Mother,,,,," she would pinch my cheek and say, "Are you talking back to your parent?" Her not allowing any back talk, no matter what it was also made me feel things were even more unfair and brought tears to my eyes, and resentment in my ungrateful heart, I would mumble to myself so as Mother could not hear me, "I wish I could die and don't you cry for me at my funeral," in my childish selfishness. (When I became a mother myself, I finally realized how much more worries and disciplinary words and actions our Mother had to go through to raise so many of us, when I was at times at a loss to raise only 3 of my children. We had a wonderful Mother, always there for us, and even in her hardship of financial burden, she never failed to say every once in a while how rich she was from having her children, and that we were her treasures. When we talked about the times we were growing up at the family parties to the grandchildren, and I talked about how lucky I am that one side of my cheek was not drooping because of the countless times Grandmother pinched it, Mother and we all could laugh about it, for some of the grandchildren were also raised by Grandma themselves, and although they were not pinched, they were told not to talk back to their parents.)

Entertainment other than the movies were the Sunday baseball games played among the various plantation teams, and our school baseball and basketball games played against other high school teams. The E.K. Fernandez carnival with their rides on the gymnasium grounds came once every so many years. Our Laupahoehoe School dances and the dances held by the community in the gym were very popular because we had a live band, "Poptown Merrymakers," with Mr. E., one of the plantation office executives, who had organized it, the band leader. Boys from our district, boys from as far as Kohala, Honokaa, Paauilo from the Hamakua coast, and boys from Hilo, Papaikou, Honomu, Hakalau, were a familiar sight at our school proms and the dances held in the Papaaloa gym, and so we girls were lucky not to be wallflowers at these dances.

Junko did the housework, cooking and sewed all of our clothes, even the trousers for the boys, which was not an easy thing for a 16-year old. She continued to sew our clothes from then on. On Father's once a year annual meeting of all the ministers, including those from the outer islands, at the Honolulu "Betsuin," he sometimes bought some ready-made outfits for us. Because our Mother had to teach Japanese school and was swamped with church work, it fell to Junko and me to take over the household chores. Of course, being the fun-loving person that I am, I ran away many times whenever I could and played with my friends like I used to when we were at Crystal City. (Junko had the most hardship among the siblings throughout our internment, taking care of all of us which continued on for many years even after coming back to Hawaii. She was a very good and kind sister and, still is. We owe her a lot for the many things she did for us as we were growing up.)

Puulai was the last village before the road started downhill towards Laupahoehoe Point. The plantation hospital was located in that area. Mr. M., the physician's assistant, at the plantation hospital was a staunch member of the temple and served also as the president of the congregation for several terms. His eldest son was the same age as Hiromichi, the second son was in the same class at school and so he went to their home and played with them, while I walked a little further up the incline behind the hospital to the Yamaoka home and played with Ronald. (As Hiromichi was 3 years younger, just as she did in the internment camp, Mother always made me go with him whenever he wanted to go to his friends' homes to play, which was usually at the Ms. and the Ishizus. I am now thinking as I write this, that perhaps, she knew that I like to play also and gave me the opportunity to do so, a break after my daily laundry duty.)

The ground of the temple was level up to where it starts to slope downward about where the left pillar of the front part of the temple stood. The hall below was the entire length and width of the temple and the first window was low, about a foot from the ground and gradually got higher as it neared the double-door entrance of the hall where the ground leveled again. The side facing the plantation garage was only slightly sloped and the windows on that side were lined without gradation. The kitchen used for the Women's Club ladies was right across from the hall, so that food could be carried easily to the tables and chairs set up for any event that served food. Wide long boards that were stored were brought out by the men, placed on wooden horses and covered with white paper cut from a big roll and taped down. People would sit on both sides of the tables facing each other at these receptions. The hall could hold four to five rows of tables lengthwise and the entire congregation could fill it. Wedding receptions, meetings, meals served after funerals, any gatherings would be held there. When weddings or funerals were held, the ladies of the temple would gather and cook the food for the reception, Mr. T. would bring the soda from his company, the wedding cake or pastries served at other events were brought by the T. bakery and every Japanese family would join in the celebration or the services without invitations. It was a close-knit community where everyone helped one another.

Now that Father was in charge of the Honohina temple, the N. family from that area came to use the hall once a week. Mr. N. was the instructor and his sons and daughter would come and learn (剣道,) "Kendo," Japanese swordsmanship, fencing from him. They wore the traditional (剣道着,) "kendogi," "kendo," uniform. Mr. N. would be wearing the "hakama" and jacket. He would call out the command of movements and the children would be in a straight row following his orders. I saw what they were doing in movies but was fascinated to actually watch them right before me. So as to not disturb or distract them, I would peek in from the low window, although I am sure they knew that I was there. The N. family was a staunch supporter of the Honohina temple and Father. (Their youngest son, F., as an adult, would become a very active supporter and leader of the Hongwanji, also served as the president of the entire Hawaii islands board.)

For one of the (敬老会,) "Keirou Kai," gatherings to respect and honor the elderly where members of the temple performed a show staged annually in the hall, Ronald and I learned "buyou" Japanese dance from his sister, Kiyomi, who had recently returned to Hawaii from Japan. We dressed in costume, wore a wig, and danced to a record. We had live music accompaniment, at these shows, U. on the guitar, T. on the ukulele, K. on the steel guitar. The young ladies, Y., F., and K., sang Japanese "Enka," (Songs of the heart of Japan.) I also sang at one of those shows. There was always a "shibai", members of the temple acting as the characters in famous stories made into plays. The elderly members always enjoyed Mr. N.'s (浪花節,) "Naniwabushi," pathetic, sentimental story sung in a manner similar to reciting, with a (三味線,) "shamisen," Japanese three-stringed banjo, strummed to a beat and emphasizing important parts of the story. The entire congregation gathered in the hall below the temple for the elderly members who were being honored and awarded gifts.

Members as cast in "shibais"

Another joyful occasion held in the summer every year was the "Bon" Dance held after the "O-bon" memorial services that honored those that have passed on. Every Buddhist temple, regardless of Sect, held "O-bon" services and "Bon" dances. The high "櫓,) "yagura," a tower built on scaffolds in the center of the temple grounds, had in it a huge drum, a phonograph and the records of the songs, (東京音頭、 霧島音頭、 炭鉱節、

安里やユンタ等）Tokyo Ondo, Kirishima Ondo, Tankou Bushi, Asatoya Yunta, etc."
choral folk songs. We danced to the music by records played on the phonograph, chanting
and singing with the beat of drums by men who originally immigrated from the prefecture
of (新潟,) "Niigata," in the (東北,) "Tohoku," Northeastern region of Japan and were now
members of our temple, everyone dancing in a ring around the "yagura." The dancers wore
a (浴衣,) "yukata," a summer kimono, and (帯,) "obi," wide sash, or a nice, dressier (着物,)
"kimono," with "obi," and (足袋,) "tabi," footwear like socks, but with a place to put the
big toe in and the rest of the toes and feet enclosed in a white cloth. This was worn when
wearing a (草履,) "zori," Japanese slipper sandals with elaborate thongs. Mother used to
dress us in "kimono" with "obi" tied into a shape of a butterfly which was appropriate for
young girls. ("Obi" was tied in styles appropriate to the women's age.) We used to go with
other members of our temple to the various Hongwanji temples and dance at their "Bon"
dances.

Bon dance

We usually ate ordinary dishes for our meals. Mother frugally planned reasonably-costing
dishes. One of the meals I did not like was preserved salted salmon, another was (おから,)
"okara," remains of the boiled soy beans left after squeezing the liquid from it to make
"tofu", soybean cake. Because the slice of fried salted salmon was very salty, we ate a lot of
rice with it which was filling. The "okara" was cooked with dried shrimp, but I always felt
that it was rather dry and not moist enough. We never had a whole steak per person, but
beef was always cut into small, thin slices and cooked with vegetables. Corn beef and
cabbage, hamburger balls with Cream of Mushroom soup as gravy, Dinner in a Dish, one of

the school lunches made with hamburger meat, onion, carrots, string beans cooked in tomato sauce, (味噌,) "Miso," soup, string beans and other boiled vegetables with mayonnaise and "shoyu" for dressing, with the "sashimi" and fried Opelu were more lavish meals for us. I really liked the par-boiled green onion tied into knots and cut into about two-inch sizes, stirred into a "Miso", sugar, vinegar sauce, which Mother made when several members brought over batches of green onion for us from their garden.

It is the custom of our Hongwanji temples, to invite guest ministers to give the sermon on special Buddhist festivals such as (花祭り "Hana-matsuri," Wesak Day, the day that Shakamuni Buddha was born, (浄土会,) "Jodo-e," Bodhi Day, when Buddha became Enlightened, (降誕会,)"Gotan-e," the day (親鸞聖人,) "Shinran Shonin,") St. Shinran, the Founder of the "Jodo Shinshu Nishi Hongwanji" Sect was born, and other festival days. On these days when the guest minister came and stayed overnight for services on Saturday evenings and on Sundays, one of the ladies from the "Fujinkai," Women's Club, would come and cook special meals for the guest minister. She would choose the menu she wanted to cook and Mother had to pay her for the cost of the meals. We looked forward to these meals for there were Macaroni or Potato salad, "sashimi", various kinds of soups, fried chicken, chicken or pork sautéed with vegetables (chop suey), steak sliced after frying, (しらあえ,) "shira ae," mashed "tofu" with boiled thinly-sliced Chinese cabbage, "Maki sushi" (Sushi rolled in seaweed), "Inari sushi" (sushi rice stuffed in fried "Tofu" shell). (As I am writing this, I can now realize that although we enjoyed these meals, it must have caused Mother some anxieties as to the costs of these favorite-menu meals cooked by each of the ladies chosen for those occasions, not knowing what dishes were to be served and how much they would cost. It must have made quite a dent into her well-planned budget. When there was left-over "sashimi" from these meals, she soaked the tuna into a sugar and vinegar sauce and made them into "Nigiri sushi" which we all enjoyed. Those days, (山葵,) "Wasabi," green horse radish, presently used when eating "sashimi" or "sushi" was not available, powdered Coleman's mustard mixed with water or grated (大根,) daikon" radish and "shoyu" were used when eating "sashimi". There were no "sushi" bars in Hawaii yet.)

The settling back to normal daily living, the familiar routines continued on in our home until March, 1951, when Father was assigned to the Main temple in Honolulu.

Looking back over those years we lived in Papaaloa Hongwanji, the years of hardships and sufferings experienced there were made bearable due to the kindness of the people that supported Father's work of ministry, which undeniably gave him the strength to raise his many children together with our Mother. Our parents never once made us feel that there were too many of us. One night, when she and I were taking a bath together, I told her that she had to suffer hardships to raise so many of us. She said that we were born because that was our destiny to be born, and that she was happy we were her children, otherwise, which child was supposed not to be born, which child was not to be our sibling. She felt blessed with her children when others who wanted children could not have them, that the Good Lord chose our parents to be given their children, and considered us their gifts and treasures.

The Matsuos, Ishizus, Teradas, Matsumuras, Tamamotos, Aokis, Ikemotos, Tanakas, Takeuchis, Furukawas, Abes, Tabatas, Uyenos, Yokomis, Jakunens, Tanakas, Takedas,Sugikawas, Yamaokas, Yamanouchis, Sugimotos, Uchimas, Adachis, Hayashidas, Shikumas, Nishimuras, Haras, Tsurudas, Yoshinas, Shimabukuro brothers, Matsushitas, Otomos, Kaneshiros, Kameis, Sakados, Yoshidas, from the Papaaloa and Laupahoehoe areas, Nonakas, Aritas, Aoyagis, Arugas, Iwahashis, Yokoyamas, Tokudas, Yamagatas, Fujiharas, Fujimoto brothers, Nishimotos, Sakamotos,Yadas, Sonodas, Uyenos (cousins to the Papaaloa Uyenos), Maedos from the Honohina and Ninole area, Higashiharas, Moris and Fukuis from the Waipunalei area, and Miuras, Nakamuras, Kobayashis, Kuniyukis, Kiyotas, Uchidas, Hoshides, Awazus, Nojiris from the Ookala area, and I am sure there were many more other families also, that made our years at the Papaaloa Hongwanji a fulfilling, memorable, and thankful assignment there. (What is also gratifying is that some of the children that attended Sunday school during those days Father was assigned to the Papaaloa and Honohina temples are now staunch supporters at the various Hongwanji Mission temples.)

For myself, the classmates and friends I made from the seventh grade, when students from Honohina, Ninole, Kaikea, Maulua, Kapehu, Papaaloa, Kihalani, Puulai, Laupahoehoe, Waipunalei and Ookala met, became close friends that still meet today, still to enjoy each other and renew our bonding as mentioned earlier in this writing. The wonderful things about growing up in a small community in the countryside, is that the entire community shares in most all celebrations, funerals, and other events, and gather to support one another, so that everyone knows what happens to each family, which makes the closeness and bonding everlasting.

My classmates, Miwako Miura Tsuruda, Itsuko Kiyota Hagino and I have met for lunch, which has become a tradition for the three of us for the last 60 plus years, in April and September, to celebrate each others' birthdays.

Itsuko, Tomoko, Miwako

Father was told by the Bishop that since his arrival to Hawaii in 1931, he had been assigned to the outer islands, but now that his older children were college-age, he was being transferred to Honolulu so that we could go to the university there. Junko had just gotten a good job as the Plantation Manager's secretary and was given a house to live in. Norie was to remain there with her. The rest of the family moved in March, 1951 to Father's new assignment at the Honpa Hongwanji Hawaii Betsuin, main temple and headquarters, in Honolulu. Just before leaving Papaaloa, Father had the family photographed in the temple.

Izumi family, 1951

CHAPTER 10

FINALLY, REDRESS AND COMPENSATION

President Ronald Reagan's approval of the redress and compensation, fought for many years by those that felt the confinement of those interned and relocated Japanese aliens and their children, even those that were American citizens, during the war was not right, and had inflicted mental suffering as well as physical suffering on all involved, finally became a reality. The bill was signed by President Reagan in 1988, but the first payment was made in October, 1990, to the eldest surviving internee.

The payments would be allotted $20,000 for the internees that met the following qualifications to be eligible to receive the restitution:
1. alive on August 10, 1988
2. United States citizen or permanent resident alien during the Internment period December 7, 1941, to June 30, 1946
3. a person of Japanese ancestry, or the spouse of parent of a person of Japanese ancestry
4. evacuated, relocated, interned, or otherwise deprived of liberty or property as a result of Federal government action during the Internment period and based solely on their Japanese ancestry

(Taken from the files for, "Check for Compensation and Reparation For the Evacuation, Relocation and Internment.")

The redress and compensation hardly make up as an apology for what we all went through, sadly, full of anxieties, and hardships of sufferings, but for many of us, it was an admission of America's having done something that was undeniably wrong to the rights of human beings and its citizens. After all, those alien Isseis were granted permanent residency by our same government and had the rights to live and own their properties, which they had worked so hard for to raise their children in the Land of Freedom. To have lost all, homes and properties taken away suddenly and unexpectedly from them, without warning, was outrageous, and unthinkably unimaginable!!

Some of the older internees did not live long enough to see this day to receive the compensation, our Father being one of them. Mother carried a photograph of Father with regret and heartache when she was called to go up and received her compensation. I cannot remember the date those of us who lived in Hawaii received our reparation compensation, but it must have been after Father passed away in January, 1990.

It was a somber and solemn occasion, and the atmosphere in that conference room in the State Capital said it all, without having any one of us internees utter a single word of complaint against America's unspeakable, irretrievable actions, which took all of us on that same road of hardships and pain. The redress and compensation brought us together on that day but for some of us, being together and seeing each other again after many years at that conference room, did not bring to our faces the joy of seeing each other again but, without any doubt, made us remember those hardship days behind the tall barbed-wired fences and guards with rifles and guns in the towers in Crystal City Internment Camp.

I am proud to be an American citizen, and I love my country. As Sumi wrote in the Crystal City Chatter, I think there are many Americans as well as Japanese Americans and people in Japan, who do not know what hardships and anxieties suffered by those that were treated as enemies in America during World War II, even some of us that were American citizens. I was inspired from the article in the Crystal City Chatter to write this wrongdoing in history as an Izumi family story, but I am sure there are many more stories yet to be told by those that shared the hardships in various other camps. It is also in hopes that such atrocities never occur again, should not occur ever again!

"Let's remember Crystal City Internment Camp!!!," a period that should not have happened to us, but one that will forever be remembered as part of our lives, and in the lives of those who were in other Relocation Camps, never, ever, to be forgotten!!!

Last photograph of the Izumi Family taken when Makoto and Tommy were still with us.

Postscript on Izumi parents and children, some deceased and others well, as of December, 2015

Father, Kakusho, deceased at age 88

Mother, Kiyo, deceased at age 83

Children:
Megumi, deceased at age 75
Junko, now 86
Takaaki, now 84
Satokazu, deceased at age 2 months
Tomoko, now 82
Hiromichi, deceased at age 44
Norie, now age 77
Makoto, deceased at age 65
Katsuyo, now 70
Thomas, deceased at age 65
Duane, now 66
Anna, our youngest sister, now 65

All of the 11 Izumi children got married, all except Hiromichi had children. 26 grandchildren, 37 great- grandchildren, 5 great-great grandchildren, 5 generations of Izumis, including our parents, (deceased,) have lived in Hawaii. The Izumi clan, children, grandchildren, great- grandchildren, great-great grandchildren, including spouses, at the present time, 2016, number 90+ members.